Technolo

Brian L. Hawkins,
Julia A. Rudy,
William H. Wallace, Jr.,
Editors

Technology Everywhere

A Campus Agenda for
Educating and Managing
Workers in the Digital Age

EDUCAUSE
Leadership Strategies No. 6

JOSSEY-BASS
A Wiley Company
www.josseybass.com

Published by

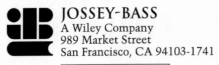

JOSSEY-BASS
A Wiley Company
989 Market Street
San Francisco, CA 94103-1741

www.josseybass.com

Copyright © 2002 by John Wiley & Sons, Inc.

Jossey-Bass is a registered trademark of John Wiley & Sons, Inc.

This book is part of the Jossey-Bass Higher and Adult Education Series.

Jossey-Bass books and products are available through most bookstores. To contact
Jossey-Bass directly, call (888) 378-2537, fax to (800) 605-2665, or visit our website at
www.josseybass.com.

Substantial discounts on bulk quantities of Jossey-Bass books are available to corporations, professional associations, and other organizations. For details and discount information, contact the special sales department at Jossey-Bass.

We at Jossey-Bass strive to use the most environmentally sensitive paper stocks available
to us. Our publications are printed on acid-free recycled stock whenever possible, and our
paper always meets or exceeds minimum GPO and EPA requirements.

Library of Congress Cataloging-in-Publication Data

Technology everywhere: a campus agenda for educating and managing workers
in the digital age / Brian L. Hawkins, Julia A. Rudy, William H. Wallace, Jr., editors.
    p. cm.—(EDUCAUSE leadership strategies; no. 6) (The Jossey-Bass
higher and adult education series)
Includes bibliographical references and index.
  ISBN 0-7879-5014-9 (pbk. : alk. paper)
   1. Education, Higher—Effect of technological innovations on—United States.
2. Information technology—United States. 3. Campus planning—United
States. I. Rudy, Julia A. II. Hawkins, Brian L. III. Wallace, William H., date–
IV. Series. V. Series: The Jossey-Bass higher and adult education series
  LB2395.7.T45 2002
  378'.00285—dc21   2002003269

PB Printing 10 9 8 7 6 5 4 3 2 1   FIRST EDITION

The EDUCAUSE Leadership Strategies series addresses critical themes related to information technology that will shape higher education in the years to come. The series is intended to make a significant contribution to the knowledge academic leaders can draw upon to chart a course for their institutions into a technology-based future. Books in the series offer practical advice and guidelines to help campus leaders develop action plans to further that end. The series is developed by EDUCAUSE and published by Jossey-Bass. The sponsorship of PricewaterhouseCoopers LLP makes it possible for EDUCAUSE to distribute complimentary copies of books in the series to more than 1,800 EDUCAUSE member institutions, organizations, and corporations.

EDUCAUSE

EDUCAUSE is a nonprofit association with offices in Boulder, Colorado, and Washington, D.C. The association's mission is to advance higher education by promoting the intelligent use of information technology. EDUCAUSE activities include an educational program of conferences, workshops, seminars, and institutes; a variety of print and on-line publications; strategic/policy initiatives such as the National Learning Infrastructure Initiative, the Net@EDU program, and the EDUCAUSE Center for Applied Research; and extensive Web-based information services.

EDUCAUSE

- provides professional development opportunities for those involved with planning for, managing, and using information technologies in colleges and universities
- seeks to influence policy by working with leaders in the education, corporate, and government sectors who have a stake in the transformation of higher education through information technologies
- enables the transfer of leading-edge approaches to information technology management and use that are developed and shared through EDUCAUSE policy and strategy initiatives
- provides a forum for dialogue between information resources professionals and campus leaders at all levels
- keeps members informed about information technology innovations, strategies, and practices that may affect their campuses, identifying and researching the most pressing issues

Current EDUCAUSE membership includes more than 1,800 campuses, organizations, and corporations. For up-to-date information about EDUCAUSE programs, initiatives, and services, visit the association's Web site at www.educause.edu, send e-mail to info@educause.edu, or call 303-449-4430.

PRICEWATERHOUSECOOPERS 🔲

PricewaterhouseCoopers is a leading provider of professional services to institutions of higher education, serving a full range of educational institutions—from small colleges to large public and private universities to educational companies.

PricewaterhouseCoopers (www.pwcglobal.com) is the world's largest professional services organization, drawing on the knowledge and skills of more than 150,000 people in 150 countries to help clients solve complex business problems and measurably enhance their ability to build value, manage risk, and improve performance in an Internet-enabled world.

PricewaterhouseCoopers refers to the member firms of the worldwide PricewaterhouseCoopers organization.

Contents

Preface

Recent literature is replete with articles and books that examine the transformational changes wrought by information technology (IT) in higher education. Previous books in the EDUCAUSE Leadership Strategies series have suggested strong campus agendas for advanced networking, e-business, knowledge management, learning marketspace partnerships, and technology-enhanced teaching and learning. In this sixth book, we turn our attention to workforce challenges in an age of ubiquitous technology.

In keeping with the goals of the series, this book offers practical advice and guidelines based on actual campus experience to help you develop a campus action plan in response to these workforce challenges. The authors we have brought together to this end explore roles for colleges and universities in the supply system for IT workers and IT-fluent workers; the need to structure campus human resource policies, practices, and roles to attract and retain the best of such workers; and the importance of developing campus IT leadership for the future.

Economic and Social Context

Before addressing these campus challenges, however, it is useful to consider several external economic and social factors that have implications for both campus administration and curriculum development.

The authors of the three chapters in Part One have engaged in significant national studies relevant to these factors; their work should go a long way toward informing and giving context to your campus planning and restructuring efforts.

IT Workforce Shortage

The second half of the last decade gave rise to a growing imbalance in the supply and demand for information technology professionals in the workforce, causing at a minimum a tight labor market for workers with certain sets of skills and in certain geographic areas by the year 2000. This was somewhat exacerbated by the high demand for information systems developers as small businesses, corporations, colleges and universities, and government agencies sought to implement or reengineer systems to survive the Y2K date rollover. With that pressure alleviated and the economic downturn and crash of many dot-com firms in 2001, more IT workers became available in the marketplace. However, an economic recovery will likely mean a resurgence of supply-and-demand challenges at some point in the future. Regardless of these fluctuations in the IT workforce overall, there is ongoing concern about underrepresentation of women and minority workers in the IT workforce.

In Chapter One, William Aspray and Peter Freeman review research conducted by the Computing Research Association on the supply of IT workers in the United States as well as a similar National Research Council study. Included in their review are definitions of an IT worker, evaluation of the supply system, discussion of shortages and market tightness, exploration of political issues, and assessment of why women and minority workers are underrepresented in the IT workforce.

Changing IT Skills and Careers

With rapid technological change now in a steady-state, the skills of IT professionals are in a continual state of flux. Fundamental changes are occurring in the information technology profession itself; new kinds of IT workers are needed as we move more deeply into the information age. This increased need for higher-level and distinctive technical skills suggests articulation and application of IT skill standards, development of new job descriptions and career clusters, and provision of just-in-time retraining as these new skills and careers emerge on the technology landscape.

In Chapter Two, Neil Evans, director of the National Workforce Center for Emerging Technologies (NWCET), examines the changing nature of skill sets and careers in the IT workforce and why there is a need for definitions and standards for IT skills. He also suggests future trends in IT skill standards and jobs in light of e-business and e-commerce; IT specialization; nontraditional IT degree paths and certifications; and IT outsourcing, contracting, and consulting.

It's Not Just About IT Workers

Information technology is revolutionizing the workplace. The nature of work is changing as new processes and styles are enabled; jobs of new sorts are created; and new kinds of employees, for whom Peter Drucker (1959) coined the term "knowledge workers," are needed. Drucker (1994) also predicted that by the end of the twentieth century, knowledge workers would make up a third or more of the U.S. workforce and new jobs would offer much greater opportunities. More recently, Thomas Davenport (1997) predicted that the "information" in information technology will take on increasing importance, creating the need for skills related to functions such as information pruning, adding context to information, enhancing the style of information, and choosing the right medium for information. And John Seely Brown believes that information navigation will be the "new form of literacy, if not the main form of literacy, for the twenty-first century" (Brown, 1999, p. 9).

These new workers require advanced education, not just technical certification or training. Their jobs, often described as "IT-enabled," require information literacy and fluency with IT. According to a report published by the National Research Council (NRC), such fluency "entails a process of lifelong learning in which individuals continually apply what they know to adapt to change and acquire more knowledge to be more effective at applying information technology to their work and personal lives" (1999, p. 2).

In Chapter Three, Herbert Lin summarizes the key findings of the NRC report, answering such questions as What is the changing nature of work in the digital age? What should everyone know about information technology to be more effective in their personal lives and in the workforce? What does IT fluency mean? He discusses the role of the college or university in promoting IT fluency and which approaches work best.

Campus Challenges: An Agenda for Change

Given this economic and social context, what are some of the resulting challenges for higher education, and how might they be met? Each chapter in Part Two of this book offers advice and recommendations from a campus perspective, in several cases based on the authors' own campus experiences. Together, these chapters represent a potential overall agenda for meeting campus workforce-related challenges in the twenty-first century.

Transforming Human Resource Management

As is the case in government and industry, human resources—people—and the intellectual capital they represent are a critical resource in higher education. Attracting and retaining these resources is coming to be recognized as fundamental to institutional success, suggesting the need to redesign the human resource (HR) infrastructure to support the mission of the institution (New Business Architecture Planning Group, 2001). There is growing recognition of the more valuable role that HR can play in knowledge- and technology-intensive environments in the corporate world (Ulrich, 1998; Roberts-Witt, 2001) as well as in higher education (Connolly, 1999).

In Chapter Four, Lauren Turner and Susan Perry urge a changing role for campus human resource organizations, emphasizing the importance of a strong partnership between HR and IT leaders and of HR playing an integral role in supporting the institutional IT agenda. They suggest a number of specific strategies that can be employed, among them being a proactive part of process and organizational change; promoting flexibility in classification, compensation, and reward systems; managing information about the IT skills and competencies of campus employees to facilitate their deployment as needed on project teams; and establishing effective training approaches and development programs. Their Mount Holyoke College case study illustrates a number of the general principles they advocate.

Recruiting, Retaining, and Retraining IT Workers

Information technology is no longer just an add-on feature for most colleges and universities; its implementation and application are increasingly mission-critical and strategic. Having the right infrastructure is crucial to attracting and retaining students, moving forward with distributed learning programs, and being able to compete with the for-profit sector in the education space. To fulfill these technology-related strategies—as well as to support the growing number of students, staff, and faculty who now depend on technology in their daily work—a higher education institution must be able to attract and retain a sufficient number of highly skilled IT professionals (Skinner and Cartwright, 1998).

In the early 1990s, college and university IT leaders began to note growing challenges in the human resource area. Among these were the need for more adequate personnel development plans and stronger career paths, the need to address IT staffing from an institutional perspective with institutional goals in mind, and the need to revisit organizational structures and processes (CAUSE Current Issues Committee, 1994). By 1999, a tight labor market for IT workers was causing an IT staffing crisis for many colleges and universities, which were hard pressed to recruit and retain IT professionals when competing with industry, where salaries and benefits were generally more lucrative (Gandel, 2000). EDUCAUSE, a nonprofit association for information technology in higher education, created a working group, in cooperation with the National Association of College and University Business Officers and the College and University Professional Association for Human Resources, to explore solutions to the crisis. The group's on-line discussions were summarized in an executive briefing, which is available on-line at www.educause.edu/pub/eb/eb1.html. EDUCAUSE also developed a Web page to identify and link to resources relevant to the intersection of HR and IT in higher education (see www.educause.edu/issues/hrit.html).

In Chapter Five, Allison Dolan offers a recipe for success in recruiting, retaining, and reskilling information technology workers that begins with establishing a strong partnership between campus IT and HR organizations. The highly practical advice in this chapter is relevant regardless of the state of the labor market for IT workers; following Dolan's guidelines can help your campus compete for and keep the best, brightest, and most skilled IT professionals, as well as develop creative retraining programs to keep them up to date in their skills.

Educating IT-Fluent and Information-Literate Workers

As proposed in the context discussion earlier in this preface, college graduates need to be fluent with IT so that they can use and apply it appropriately in their work in the information society. In an interview with the *Chronicle of Higher Education*, Rita Colwell related the National Science Foundation's concern about "having students who really are capable, not just computer-literate, but highly versatile." The NSF, she said, is "looking for ways to update curricula, to enrich courses with technology" (Carnevale, 2001, p. A50).

The pressing need to produce IT-fluent graduates (especially liberal arts majors) for today's workforce demands that colleges and universities consider significant curriculum change. What are the challenges and key issues that arise in developing curriculum to ensure IT-fluent and information-literate graduates? What are the partnerships on campus that are necessary for such programs to be successful? In Chapter Six, Anne Scrivener Agee and John Zenelis draw on their experience with George Mason University's award-winning Technology Across the Curriculum Program to share the ten factors they have found to be crucial elements in implementing a successful program. Critical among these are institutionwide engagement and buy-in and collaboration among many campus stakeholders, especially the library and IT units.

Partnering to Close the Gap

One primary characteristic of the IT industry is rapid change; workers with up-to-date ("hot") and highly specialized technology skills are critical to the product development cycles of many corporations. Such workers are not necessarily—perhaps even not likely to be—the product of a traditional, four-year undergraduate education. Some corporations (Cisco and Microsoft are good examples) have developed certification programs to ensure rapid training of specifically skilled IT workers.

An emerging trend, however, could be a new paradigm for the future: the partnering of colleges and universities with corporations to offer hybrid programs combining traditional education with more skills-related training on a faster track. A September 5, 2001, *Edupage* abstract reported that a U.S. Department of Education study predicts colleges and universities will continue to develop such hybrid certification programs through private industry alliances as a way of generating revenue and meeting changing corporate and student needs. Although it is not the business of higher education to "churn out graduates with hot skills," a recent *CIO Magazine* article concluded that colleges and universities can collaborate with corporations to produce the kind of IT worker they are looking for (Compton, 2001).

In Chapter Seven, Annie Hunt Burriss and William Wallace explore the concept of partnering in economic development efforts with other institutions, industry, and government agencies to address the IT skills gap, as well as attract IT-related industry to a specific geographic region. They describe several successful partnerships that the state of Georgia has implemented and the key factors that have contributed to their success.

Ensuring Strong Campus IT Leadership

As they work to effectively integrate information technology into the fabric of their institution, campus leaders are struggling more than ever with structural, operational, and governance issues. In particular, they are challenged to find the right kind of leadership for IT (Hawkins and Rudy, 2001). A vital issue for any college or university is finding a way to talk usefully about just what constitutes leadership in the context of information technology in higher education (Warger, 2001).

In Chapter Eight, Brian Hawkins and Deanna Marcum present such "useful talk." They discuss the need to define a new leadership role for campus information resource and technology administrators, suggesting that campus leadership for IT must become a shared responsibility among key administrators (including the chief information officer) to ensure that IT plans and directions are aligned with institutional goals and mission. After recommending a set of strategies for effective technology leadership, they raise the critical question about where leaders with such appropriate skills, competencies, and perspectives will come from in the future.

Conclusion

The IT staffing crisis in higher education may have temporarily subsided, but with the central role that technology will continue to play in our society, it is foolhardy to suggest that it has been adequately addressed. There once was a time when the IT skills called for in higher education were unique and not really transferable to other arenas in the for-profit sector. It made sense for a college or university to think it had a captive market, to pay commensurately lower salaries, and to depend on the qualities of the campus environment (flexibility, innovation, and exciting new technologies) to alternatively compensate IT staff. Those days are now history.

Today, campus administrators, trustees, and IT and HR administrators alike must seek new, adaptive, and creative strategies to recruit and retain the staff needed to support the new technologies that are so strategic to all dimensions of the higher education enterprise. This requires new policies; new approaches to compensation; creativity in seeking from nontraditional sources those with IT skills; and most of all a collaborative approach, with HR professionals, IT professionals, and academic and administrative leaders all working together in a focused effort on these challenges.

Most of all, this new collaboration requires a new commitment to training, developing, and upgrading the skills of these professionals. Throughout most of the last half of the twentieth century, higher education had a less-than-distinguished record when it came to systematically investing in the professional development of staff in general, and IT staff development in particular. This must change if retention of quality staff is to occur.

Dynamic changes in technology are occurring at such a pace that constant upgrading of the skills of IT staff is clearly a concomitant requirement. In most cases, this entails significant change in campus budgeting and planning. Investment in professional development also needs to recognize that the career ladder in information technology requires a shift from specialized technical skills at an entry-level position to broad, general management, and collaborative skills at the most senior positions.

We hope this book can precipitate necessary campus discussion on the current state of staffing, curriculum, and training as well as

the policies and programs necessary to ensure a stable yet dynamic
IT environment to support the institutional mission. If this dialogue
alone occurs, we will have succeeded in our purpose.

February 2002   BRIAN L. HAWKINS
                                                    JULIA A. RUDY
                                            WILLIAM H. WALLACE, JR.

References

Brown, J. S. "Learning, Working, and Playing in the Digital Age." Presentation
    at American Association of Higher Education Conference, Mar. 1999,
    Washington, D.C. [Transcript at http://www.ntlf.com/html/sf/jsbrown.pdf]

Carnevale, D. "Science Foundation's Director Sees Equity and Access as Major
    Technology Issues." *Chronicle of Higher Education*, Nov. 2, 2001, p. A50.
    [chronicle.com/free/2001/10/2001101901t.htm]

CAUSE Current Issues Committee. "Current Issues in Higher Education
    Information Technology." *CAUSE/EFFECT*, Spring 1994, pp. 3–5.
    [www.educause.edu/ir/library/text/cem9412.txt]

Compton, J. "How to Take Over the Classroom." *CIO Magazine*, Nov. 1, 2001.
    [www.cio.com/archive/110101/classroom.html]

Connolly, T. R. "Transforming Human Resources in Higher Education." In
    D. Oblinger and R. Katz (eds.), *Renewing Administration: Preparing Colleges
    and Universities for the 21st Century*. Bolton, Mass.: Anker, 1999.

Davenport, T. H. *Information Ecology: Mastering the Information and Knowledge
    Environment*. New York: Oxford University Press, 1997.

Drucker, P. *Landmarks of Tomorrow: A Report on the New "Post-Modern" World*.
    New York: HarperCollins, 1959.

Drucker, P. "The Age of Social Transformation." *Atlantic Monthly*, Nov. 1994,
    pp. 53–80. [www.theatlantic.com/politics/ecbig/soctrans.htm]

Edupage. "University of IT." Sept. 5, 2001. [listserv.educause.edu/archives/
    edupage.html]

Gandel, P. "Top Ten IT Challenges of 2000." *EDUCAUSE Quarterly*, 2000,
    23(2), 10–13. [www.educause.edu/ir/library/pdf/eq/a002a.pdf]

Hawkins, B. L., and Rudy, J. A. "Stalking the Elusive, Venerated IT Worker."
    Trusteeship, Jan.–Feb. 2001, pp. 32–35.

National Research Council, Committee on Information Technology Literacy.
    Being Fluent with Information Technology. Washington, D.C.: National
    Academy Press, 1999. [books.nap.edu/books/030906399X/
    html/index.html]

New Business Architecture Planning Group. *UC 2010: A New Business Architecture*. Oakland: University of California, 2001. [uc2010.ucsd.edu]

Roberts-Witt, S. L. "Reinventing HR." *Knowledge Management Magazine*, Sept. 2001. [www.destinationcrm.com/km/dcrm_km_article.asp?id=958]

Skinner, R. A., and Cartwright, G. P. "Higher Education and the Technology Workforce Shortage." *Change*, May/June 1998, pp. 52–55.

Ulrich, D. "A New Mandate for Human Resources." *Harvard Business Review*, 1998, 76(1), 124–134.

Warger, T. "Leadership: Connecting Vision to Action." *EDUTECH Report*, Aug. 2001, pp. 4–5.

Acknowledgments

First and foremost, we would like to thank the authors who contributed their time and expertise to the development of this book. We appreciate their willingness to help us deliver their research summaries, insights, and lessons learned to inform a "people" agenda for college and university leaders in an increasingly digital future.

The creation and delivery of volumes in the EDUCAUSE Leadership Strategies series reflect the commitment of the EDUCAUSE board of directors and members to advancing higher education by promoting the intelligent use of information technology (IT). Such use depends greatly on development and management of the IT workers and IT-fluent workers who are critical to supporting the new technologies and the innovative strategies they enable for the higher education enterprise—thus the decision to focus this sixth volume on IT-related people challenges.

We also wish to express our appreciation to the dedicated group of IT professionals, human resource professionals, and business officers who three years ago identified and discussed major HR challenges related to IT on college and university campuses. Their work, which was part of an effort sponsored by EDUCAUSE in cooperation with CUPA-HR (College and University Professional Association for Human Resources) and NACUBO (National Association of College and University Business Officers), laid the foundation for our further exploration of such challenges in this book.

Finally, we thank PricewaterhouseCoopers for their generous sponsorship of the EDUCAUSE Leadership Strategies series, which ensures the distribution of each volume to more than 1,800 EDUCAUSE representatives at member campuses, organizations, and corporations.

B.L.H.
J.A.R.
W.H.W.

The Authors

Brian L. Hawkins is president of EDUCAUSE. Previously he was chief information officer and later senior vice president for academic planning and administrative affairs at Brown University. Prior to that, he was associate vice president for academic affairs at Drexel University, where he was responsible for general academic planning and also oversaw the academic program that was the first in the nation to require student access to a microcomputer and to integrate technology use throughout the curriculum. Hawkins is a management professor by training and author of three books and many articles in organizational behavior and technology and academic planning. He received bachelor's and master's degrees from Michigan State University and a Ph.D. from Purdue University.

Julia A. Rudy is director of product development at EDUCAUSE. Previously she was director of research and development and editor of *EDUCAUSE Quarterly* and director of publications and editor of the journal *CAUSE/EFFECT* for more than seventeen years at CAUSE. She has served as series editor of the EDUCAUSE Leadership Strategies series, published by Jossey-Bass, since its inception. Rudy is a coauthor of *Campus Financial Systems for the Future* (1996) and coeditor of *Information Technology in Higher Education: Assessing Its Impact and Planning for the Future* (1999). She is a graduate of Duquesne University, where she received a B.A. in English literature.

William H. Wallace, Jr., is associate vice chancellor for human resources for the University System of Georgia, responsible for managing all employee benefit programs providing coverage for the employees, retirees, and dependents of the system's thirty-four member institutions. Previously he was director of human resources at Kennesaw State University and assistant director of human resources at Georgia Southern University. Over the past few years, Wallace has had a special interest and engaged in research regarding recruitment and retention of information technology workers. He has been an active member, regionally and nationally, of the College and University Professional Association for Human Resources. He received an M.P.A. in public administration and a B.S. in political science from Georgia Southern University.

Anne Scrivener Agee is executive director of the Division of Instructional and Technology Support Services and deputy chief information officer at George Mason University. She is responsible for coordinating the university's technology integration initiatives, including program planning as well as faculty and student support and training. In particular, she has worked with the College of Arts and Sciences at George Mason to develop the Technology Across the Curriculum program, winner of the 2001 EDUCAUSE award for systemic progress in teaching and learning. She is a fellow of the Frye Institute for Leadership in Information Technology, inaugural class of 2000. She holds an M.A. in English from Ohio University and a doctorate in rhetoric from the Catholic University of America.

William Aspray is executive director of the Computing Research Association, an educational nonprofit association of more than 190 North American academic departments of computer science, computer engineering, and related fields; laboratories and centers in industry, government, and academia engaging in basic computing research; and affiliated professional societies. Previously he taught mathematical sciences at Williams College and history of science at Harvard University. He also served as director of the Institute of Electrical and Electronic Engineering History Center at Rutgers University and associate director of the Charles Babbage Institute at the University of Minnesota. Aspray writes on historical and contemporary issues concerning computing research, with special interest in workforce issues, professionalization, computing as an academic discipline, and research funding and organizations. He received bachelor's and master's degrees in mathematics from Wesleyan University and a Ph.D. in the history of science from the University of Wisconsin.

Annie Hunt Burriss is assistant vice chancellor for economic development at the Georgia Board of Regents, University System of Georgia. Under her leadership, the Intellectual Capital Partnership Program (ICAPP®) has received national recognition for developing sustainable intellectual capital resources through market-driven partnerships between education and business. For seventeen years, Burriss has served as an economic development professional in the public and private sectors. She was Georgia's first woman to earn credentials as a Certified Economic Developer and is past president of the Georgia Economic Developers Association. She earned fine arts degrees from Sullins College and Stephens College and a master's degree in city planning from Georgia Tech, and she has completed advanced studies at the Wharton School of the University of Pennsylvania.

Allison F. Dolan is director of information technology staff development and resource management at the Massachusetts Institute of Technology (MIT), responsible for recruiting, retention, and related human resource issues for the information systems (IS) department, working in collaboration with MIT's central human resource department. She is also responsible for overseeing intra-IS financial and administrative services. Prior to joining MIT, Dolan had twenty-two years of experience at Eastman Kodak, where she was director of an organization that provided heterogeneous system administration and desktop support to dozens of departments. She is a member of the Society for Human Resource Management. She received a B.A. with a double major in computer science and economics from the University of Delaware.

Neil Evans is executive director of the National Workforce Center for Emerging Technologies, an affiliation of Bellevue Community College and twelve National Science Foundation Advanced Technology Education Centers of Excellence. NWCET is nationally recognized as a leader in delivering innovative solutions for information technology education. Previously, Evans was dean of information resources at Bellevue Community College and chief information officer at Microsoft for ten years. He was recognized for three years by *CIO Magazine* as among the nation's one hundred leading information technology officers. He has presented at national and international conferences, including the Vice President's Conference on Jobs for the 21st Century Economy and the National IT Workforce Convocation. He holds a B.A. from Northwestern University and an M.B.A. from Northwestern's Kellogg Graduate School of Management.

Peter A. Freeman is the John P. Imlay, Jr., Dean and Professor in the College of Computing at Georgia Institute of Technology. Before going to Georgia Tech, he held positions at George Mason University; University of California, Irvine; and the National Science Foundation. He coauthored *The Supply of Information Technology Workers in the United States* (1999) and authored *Software Perspectives: The System is the Message* (1987) and *Software Systems Principles* (1975). In addition, he edited or coedited four books and has published many technical papers. He is a member of the board of directors of the Computing Research Association and a fellow of the Institute of Electrical and Electronic Engineering, the Association for Computing Machinery, and the Association for the Advancement of Science. He received his Ph.D. in computer science from Carnegie-Mellon University.

Herbert S. Lin is senior scientist and senior staff officer at the Computer Science and Telecommunications Board, National Research Council (NRC) of the National Academies. He has been the study director of major projects on public policy and information technology, including a 1996 study on national cryptography policy; a 1991 study on the future of computer science; a 1999 study of Defense Department systems for command, control, communications, computing, and intelligence; and a 2000 study on workforce issues in high technology. Prior to his NRC service, he was a professional staff member and staff scientist for the House Armed Services Committee, where his portfolio included defense policy and arms control issues. He also has significant expertise in math and science education. He received his doctorate in physics from the Massachusetts Institute of Technology.

Deanna B. Marcum is president of the Council on Library and Information Resources, whose mission is to identify the critical issues that affect the welfare and prospects of libraries and archives and the constituencies they serve, convene individuals and organizations in the best position to engage these issues and respond to them, and encourage institutions to work collaboratively to achieve and manage change. She has served as director of public service and collection management at the Library of Congress, dean of the School of Library and Information Science at the Catholic University of America, and program officer and then vice president of the Council on Library Resources. She holds a Ph.D. in American studies, a master's degree in library science, and a bachelor's degree in English.

Susan Perry is a senior adviser to the Andrew W. Mellon Foundation, working with the National Institute for Technology and Liberal Education to help Mellon-supported liberal arts colleges with issues regarding teaching and learning with technology. She is also director of programs for the Council on Library and Information Resources.

Previously she was director of Library, Information and Technology Services at Mount Holyoke College. She also held leadership positions in libraries and computing centers at Stanford University and Evergreen State College. Her information management experience covers libraries, academic computing, administrative computing, and media services. Perry serves on the faculty of the EDUCAUSE Leadership Institute, the board of directors of EDUCAUSE, and the steering committee for the Coalition for Networked Information. She received an undergraduate degree in history from Wake Forest University and an M.S. degree in library science from the University of North Carolina, Chapel Hill.

Lauren A. Turner is director of human resources and affirmative action at Mount Holyoke College, where she is responsible for oversight of all human resource functions, including recruitment, salary administration, employee and labor relations, benefits, HR information systems, and payroll. She is an active member of the College and University Professional Association for Human Resources (CUPA-HR), having served on its strategic planning committee and other program planning committees and presented at numerous CUPA-HR regional and national conferences. She has also served as president of the Southern New England regional chapter of CUPA-HR and is a continuing member of its steering committee. Turner received her B.S. in human resources from the University of Massachusetts, Amherst, and her M.A. in psychology from Mount Holyoke College.

John G. Zenelis is university librarian and associate vice president for information technology at George Mason University. Previously he held administrative positions in the libraries at Temple University and Columbia University. He began his professional career at the Research Libraries, New York Public Library. Zenelis is a member of the steering committee of VIVA, the Virtual Library of Virginia, and of Virginia's State Council of Higher Education Library Advisory

Council; he is actively involved with regional and national library consortia and professional associations. He received a B.A. in political science from Temple University, an M.L.S. from the University of Pittsburgh, and an M.A. in political science from the City University of New York, and he completed doctoral studies in educational administration at Temple University.

Part I

The Context

1

The Supply of IT Workers in the United States

William Aspray, Peter A. Freeman

What is the nature of information technology (IT) workers? Where do they come from? What are some of the political and economic factors and supply issues that are most relevant to an educational institution? The breadth and depth of the higher education system in the United States makes it impossible in this brief chapter to do more than offer a broad sketch of the supply of IT workers in the United States. Yet our experience has been that even a modicum of scholarly rigor can serve to clarify many important discussions that otherwise seem to bog down.

What Is an IT Worker?

In answering the question of what an IT worker is, there are three definitional types to consider: labor-category, skill-set, and work-related.

A *labor-category* definition, such as those used by the U.S. Bureau of Labor Statistics, is necessary for comparison, regulatory purposes, devising specific training programs, and so on. However, the Standard Occupational Categories (SOC) currently used by the BLS are essentially a distillation of job titles, an increasingly out-of-date and inaccurate reflection of what people do or the skills they need. Thus we believe this type of definition, in general, is deeply flawed for understanding strategic issues and for planning.

A *skill-set* definition (what should a worker of type X be able to do?) is obviously useful in devising a training program and helpful in some ways in building or modifying a broader educational program. There is some obvious overlap between skill-set definition and labor-category definition, which is one thing that reduces the broad usefulness of the former. The biggest impediment in our opinion is that it is generally impossible to predict in detail what skill sets will be needed in the future—even next year.

We took the *work-related* approach in a Computing Research Association (CRA) study three years ago (Freeman and Aspray, 1999), returning to basics and looking at the fundamentals of what people are *doing* in their work, independent of the job title or skill set. This permitted us to consider strategic questions much more easily. A recent National Research Council study (Committee on Workforce Needs in Information Technology, 2000) also gave some consideration to fundamentals, but to be able to consider federal data in detail, it basically used a labor-category approach.

Our CRA study report presents a discussion of these definitional types and some previous attempts to define IT workers and then proposes a work-related definition. We extract liberally from that report in the discussion that follows.

A Four-Category Approach (CRA Study)

There are two categorizations that can help with planning and estimation. The first distinguishes IT workers from other kinds who may sometimes use information technology in their jobs. In Figure 1.1, each IT-related occupation is located at a single point on the graph. As one moves from left to right, the occupations require an increasing amount of IT knowledge. As one moves from bottom to top, the occupations require an increasing amount of domain knowledge (knowledge of business practice, industry practice, technical practice, or other kind of knowledge particular to an application domain). The diagonal line separates the IT-related occupations into two classes, depending on whether IT knowledge or domain knowledge is more important. If more than half the value provided by a worker involves his or her IT knowledge, then this person is considered to be an *IT worker*. If the person's occupation involves using information technology but it contributes less than half the value added to the work, then we regard the person as an *IT-enabled worker*. A few occupations are plotted on the figure as examples.

The second categorization focuses only on the IT workers. Exhibit 1.1 differentiates four categories of IT worker, depending on the principal functionality in the occupation. The exhibit includes examples of particular IT occupations that fall under each category: conceptualizers, developers, modifiers/extenders, and supporters/tenders.

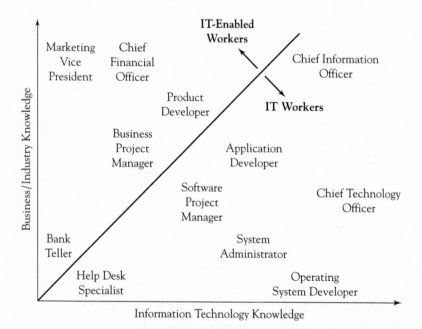

Figure 1.1. Distinguishing IT Workers from IT-Enabled Workers

Source: Computing Research Association, Intersociety Study Group on Information Technology Workers, published in Freeman and Aspray, 1999.

Exhibit 1.1. Categorization of IT Jobs

Conceptualizers are those who conceive of and sketch out the basic nature of a computer system artifact:

- Entrepreneur
- Product designer
- Research engineer
- Systems analyst
- Computer science researcher
- Requirements analyst
- System architect

Developers are those who work on specifying, designing, constructing, and testing an information technology artifact:

- System designer
- Programmer
- Software engineer
- Tester
- Computer engineer
- Microprocessor designer
- Chip designer

Modifiers/extenders are those who modify or add on to an information technology artifact:

- Maintenance programmer
- Programmer
- Software engineer
- Computer engineer
- Database administrator

Supporters/tenders are those who deliver, install, operate, maintain, or repair an information technology artifact:

- System consultant
- Customer support specialist
- Help desk specialist
- Hardware maintenance specialist
- Network installer
- Network administrator

Source: Computing Research Association, Intersociety Study Group on Information Technology Workers, published in Freeman and Aspray, 1999.

The categorization is built from a developmental perspective of the world. It is based on experience and familiarity with the IT industry, where the workers are responsible for creating IT artifacts. However, this categorization applies reasonably well to all kinds of IT worker in all sectors of the economy, including universities.

We believe there is a reasonably good match between level of formal education and category of worker. Table 1.1 maps formal education onto the four categories. There is no exact one-to-one

Table 1.1. Typical Educational Preparation for IT Jobs

	Highest Degree Attained				
	High School Diploma	Associate Degree	Bachelor's Degree	Master's Degree	Doctorate
Conceptualizers	✓	✓	✔	✔	✔
Developers			✔	✔	✓
Modifiers		✓	✔	✔	✓
Supporters	✓	✔	✔		

Note: Blank cell = unlikely; ✓ = occasional; ✔ = common; ✔ = frequent.

Source: Computing Research Association, Intersociety Study Group on Information Technology Workers, published in Freeman and Aspray, 1999.

correspondence between educational degree and category of work; however, the table clearly shows a correlation. (This correlation breaks down in the case of the earliest stage of conceptualization of an IT system, where the initial functional idea often comes from people with little IT education but great application knowledge.) Occupations that fall under the *conceptualizer* category are commonly populated with recipients of a master's degree or doctorate. Occupations that fall under the *developer* or *modifier* categories are usually filled by people with a bachelor's or master's degree—and in the case of the modifier category, sometimes by a person with an associate's degree. Supporter occupations tend to be filled most commonly with people holding an associate's degree, or perhaps only a high school diploma.

A Two-Category Approach (NRC Study)

The 2000 National Research Council study, *Building a Workforce for the Information Economy*, also returns to the fundamentals of the work done, in a fashion similar to our study. The NRC study group differentiates between IT workers and those whose primary job is *enabled* by using IT. Thus they define IT workers as "those persons engaged primarily in the conception, design, development, adaptation, implementation, deployment, training, support, documentation, and management of information technology systems, components, or applications" (p. 44).

After careful examination, the study committee found that two categories were sufficient for their analysis. Work in category one involves "the development, creation, specification, design, and testing of an IT artifact, or the development of system-wide applications for services; it also involves IT research" and thus corresponds broadly to the categories of *conceptualizer* and *developer* in the CRA study. Category two work primarily involves the "application, adaptation, configuration, support, or implementation of IT products or services designed or developed by others" and thus corresponds to the categories *modifier/extender* and *supporter/tender*.

The NRC study does a good job of explicating the interaction between these categories of work, the skill and knowledge requirements for various types of worker, and the nature of the existing workforce. If your need for a categorization system is deep, then we recommend that you read the NRC study (at least its second chapter). If your need is less detailed, then either categorization scheme serves as a framework for analysis and planning.

Which scheme you use is probably dictated by what you are trying to achieve. Trying to plan for the proper balance of academic programs on a campus, for example, is likely to be well served by the (slightly) more detailed scheme of the CRA report. An early field test of the scheme for this purpose has substantiated its usefulness. On the other hand, if you are simply trying to determine which jobs on a campus should be placed on an "in short supply" list, then the two-category scheme of the NRC report is probably sufficient.

The Supply System

As we suggested in our study report (Freeman and Aspray, 1999), the traditional, formal educational system remains critically important to the supply of IT workers. Jobs of various kinds within the IT field, however, require quite different skill sets and levels of knowledge; thus IT jobs vary greatly in the kind and level of education they require. This is a critical point that was often largely overlooked in the early days of the IT boom, when we heard calls for producing hundreds of thousands of highly educated people. What was actually needed was an increase in the supply of a range of workers, most of whom did not need extensive education.

Formal programs leading to associate's, bachelor's, master's, and doctoral degrees in IT-related fields all have their place in the supply system. An associate degree trains a person for certain kinds of entry-level position that may involve maintaining or tending IT products, whereas a doctorate might prepare a person to create entirely new information technologies. None of the relations between training, education, and particular IT occupations are hard and fast, though.

Associate's and master's degree programs are an important supply source for IT workers because they tend to be more vocationally oriented than bachelor's or doctoral programs. However, bachelor's degree programs have produced the largest number of graduates for the IT workforce, and the doctoral programs are critical in producing trained workers for occupations involving conceptualization and advanced development as well as faculty positions that educate the next generation of IT workers. The most popular IT-related major is computer science, followed by computer engineering and management information systems. However, one author has identified twenty IT-related degree disciplines offered in the United States, and new ones are being created all the time (Denning, 1998). What these programs teach is more important than what they are called. Indeed, program names are often confusing, and it can be difficult to establish similarity or difference between programs solely on the basis of their names.

One of the least known yet most important facts is that the vast majority of IT workers do not obtain a formal degree in an IT-related discipline. Perhaps the most common of the many training paths to an IT career is a bachelor's degree in some technical field nominally unrelated to information technology, accompanied by some course work in either an IT subject or a closely related preparatory field, such as mathematics, electrical engineering, or business.

We would note, however, that the scene is changing rapidly. The proliferation of new majors, and options in existing majors, now give many students a variety of choices. Students and counselors now better understand that one does not always need a computer science or computer engineering degree to enter the IT field and succeed. Traditional majors—such as electrical engineering, industrial engineering, or operations research—are in some cases morphing into majors that essentially produce IT workers.

All of this means that the earlier statements about where most IT workers come from may be obsolete in a few years. More important, in a pluralistic and decentralized university where an individual department can more or less redefine itself and its majors, any attempt at central planning is difficult at best.

At the same time, certain IT occupations do demand a particular kind of formal education. An advanced researcher, such as a faculty member in a research university or a principal scientist in an industrial research laboratory, almost always has a doctorate in an IT-related discipline, usually computer science or computer engineering (or occasionally in a closely related field, such as physics, mathematics, psychology, or electrical engineering).

Over the past decade, there have been vast changes in the characteristics of IT work and preparation for it. Traditionally, higher education served as the basis for one's career, although some of the larger IT companies had training programs for their employees. Today, higher education is an entry ramp into a job, but it is not expected to carry one through a career. Taking advantage of on-the-job experience and various kinds of continuing education, the IT employee is today expected to engage in a life-long retraining effort, which is intended to keep the worker up to date in this rapidly changing field.

Many groups supply this continuing education. The higher educational system has a major role, offering seminars, short courses, and groups of courses that lead to a certificate in a specialized aspect of information technology such as network administration or biocomputing. Universities often attract the mid-career employee who goes back to earn an additional degree, perhaps a computer science degree for someone who majored in humanities or a master's degree in business administration for the computer engineer. Every level of the higher education system participates, but the training is most likely to come at the associate or master's level.

Others provide continuing education and retraining as well. For-profit educational companies, such as DeVry or the University of Phoenix, offer formal degree programs and certificate programs. Private consultants and private training companies offer specialized seminars, as well as customized training programs for individual companies. Companies themselves are getting into the training business for their own employees (and sometimes for others), forming "corporate universities" that they may develop on their own or in partnership with one of the other traditional or for-profit suppliers. The corporate university not only teaches IT technical materials but also develops communications and interpersonal skills and imparts knowledge of business and industry practices. It is believed that there are between fifteen hundred and two thousand corporate universities today, in addition to countless training departments.

The need for continual retraining has made it necessary to rethink how education is delivered. It has to be made available at a time and place, and in a style, that accommodates the employee's work and personal life. This requires more frequent offerings on evenings and weekends, scattered around numerous geographical locations. Even better, in some cases, is use of teaching methods that free the student from a specific time and place. Computer, Internet, and broadcast technologies are being used to develop various kinds of distance learning, some of which can be engaged by the student asynchronously—that is, when the student wants the training, not when a teacher is scheduled to give a lecture. These technologies are available in a rudimentary form today, but their development continues and they are being put into practice at a rapid pace.

It is clear that distance learning offers some interesting new approaches, but just where and how to use them is not clear at all. Predictions of the imminent demise of the traditional university because of these new technologies have proven to be premature, while at the same time the plethora of experimentation with new approaches has yet to show us the best way to proceed. Because of the demand for people and the expectation that IT students should be more comfortable with technological approaches, the supply system for IT workers is a primary laboratory for distance learning.

The university has traditionally been where people turned for continuing education, and even distance education (remember correspondence courses?). But the newer providers in many cases have taken the lead in offering this much-needed (and profitable) service to IT workers and those who want to be IT workers. In some areas, this is entirely appropriate (a research university should not be wasting resources teaching low-level skills), but in other areas the university is now scrambling to remain relevant.

Shortages and Market Tightness

There has been a great deal of discussion over the past several years of a shortage of IT workers in the United States. Various studies, such as those released by the Information Technology Association of America (ITAA) and the Department of Commerce, quantify the size of that shortage—typically in the hundreds of thousands of people. These claims have been used as principal evidence when companies and industry trade associations have requested changes in immigration law to allow more foreign IT workers to enter the United States. Yet the CRA and NRC studies on IT workers have found that the evidence for a shortage is less than compelling. These studies instead point to tightness in the labor market.

According to the Department of Labor definition, a *shortage* occurs when there is a disequilibrium between supply and demand. Thus, to be able to claim a shortage, one must be able to count the supply and the demand with reasonable precision and demonstrate that there is a greater demand than supply. Unfortunately, this task presents several serious challenges to the objective analyst.

First, there are problems with defining an IT worker—no matter which definition one chooses to use. Many jobs are borderline as to whether they are IT or not, and companies respond to surveys differently when they count IT workers. Many surveys focus only on workers needed for the IT industry; others are broader. Thus it is hard to get a count on the number of filled and unfilled IT jobs on the demand side.

There is also a problem in counting the supply. There are reasonably accurate figures on the number of people who graduate each year with various formal degrees—from associate through doctorate—in computing-related fields (computer science, computer engineering, management information science, and so forth). However, historically only a small percentage of IT workers received a formal degree in the field, and there is little reason to believe this will change any time soon. In fact, the supply pool comes from many sources, only a small part of which is determined by formal education.

Another problem is that supply and demand are not necessarily measured most effectively at the national level. If there were an excess of IT workers in Boston and a deficit of IT workers in San Francisco, it would not necessarily mean that the labor markets in the two places would equalize. There are often constraints on the ability and interest of IT workers to relocate from one part of the country to another.

Not only is there geographical segregation of the IT labor market, there is also job-type segregation. IT work encompasses a large number of jobs with wide variability in the skill set and knowledge required to do the work. Some jobs require an advanced computer science degree; there are others (as at a computer help desk) for which a computer science doctorate would be ill-suited. Thus, in figuring out the actual market place match between supply and demand, one cannot legitimately talk about IT work as a whole but instead must talk about various jobs.

There are also problems with the data. The federal data tend to be the most complete and objective, but often several years out of date—much too old for use in making decisions in this rapidly changing field. Supply data from the Department of Education are hard to match up with demand and employment data from the Bureau of Labor. Some national data, such as those supplied by the Department of Commerce and the ITAA, have been called into question on methodological grounds (small sample size, how the data were collected). It is hard to generalize from location-specific or occupation-specific statistical studies, such as those of the Washington Software Alliance.

For these reasons and others, the CRA and NRC studies both claim that we have insufficient evidence to assert there is actually a shortage of IT workers in the United states, much less to quantify that shortage.

Both the CRA and NRC studies do, however, observe tightness in the market. Evidence is in a variety of corporate actions (more recruiting, increase in salaries and benefits, more contracting out of IT work) and greater job churning (that is, growth in the number of resignations and hirings as IT workers hop from one job to another). Beyond this tightness in the labor market, it is hard to make any claims.

Political Issues

Because of the cries from industry over the past several years, legislators at the local, state, and especially the federal levels have been seeking political means to increase the IT labor pool. There have been state-funded regional efforts at economic development, such as the successful Yamacraw project in Georgia, which include workforce development. There are programs, such as one in northern Virginia to increase the production of low-end IT workers through increased access to an associate's degree, especially for people who previously were on the disadvantaged side of the Digital Divide. The final results of these programs for low-end workers are not yet in, but they seem to have had at best mixed success. Attempts have been made at the state and federal levels to give tax relief to companies that offer training for technical workers. This legislation may have a chance of success at the state level, but it is unlikely to be passed at the federal level.

Employers want more workers now, not sometime in the distant future. Thus political attention has been focused primarily on short-term solutions. Some federal agencies, such as the National Science Foundation, the Department of Education, and the Department of Commerce, have worked on Digital Divide and K–12 and higher education programs to a limited extent. There has also been modest focus on underrepresented groups such as women and some ethnic minorities. But the main focus has been on a quick fix—in particular on immigration.

The immigration issue has focused primarily on the H-1B visa program. The H-1B is a temporary visa that resulted from some major legislative changes in U.S. immigration law of the 1980s and is modeled after a temporary visa program (H-1A) for nurses of 1989. The H-1A program, incidentally, proved to be of only short-term success in alleviating the nursing shortage, and then only for a few regions (notably New York City).

The H-1B program enables specialty occupation workers such as foreign specialty cooks, physical therapists, fashion models, and high-tech workers to enter the United States. In the first half of the 1990s, no more than about twenty-five thousand high-tech workers entered the United States under this program each year. In the late 1990s, the demand for IT workers under this program grew dramatically, and the annual cap of 65,000 visas was reached well before the end of the federal fiscal year. Two later revisions of the

H-1B legislation raised the cap (it is now 195,000). The revisions also include two exemptions from the cap that have a special impact on universities: for those who hold a graduate degree and those who are employed in a university.

There are many problems with the H-1B visa program. Many people have criticized the management of the program by the Immigration and Naturalization Service for delays in processing applications and inability to keep track of how many H-1B visas have been awarded in a given year. Many of the workers who enter the United States under this temporary visa program would like to remain here permanently, and many apply for a permanent visa. Unfortunately, these new applications for permanent visa exacerbate an already overtaxed INS; the typical applicant waits many years for a decision on permanent visa status—often not receiving a decision before the temporary visa expires.

Labor unions and some groups supporting minorities and the elderly have been opposed to the H-1B program, noting that these visas take safe, high-paying, high-skill jobs out of the hands of American workers. These criticisms have been somewhat louder over the past year, in the wake of the dot-com crash. Others have criticized the program because it removes the incentive to find a long-term solution to ramping up our educational system to produce an adequate number of indigenous American IT workers, and that it does not force the country to find ways to better enfranchise underrepresented groups.

For an immigration strategy to work, there must be qualified IT workers in other countries willing to come to the United States. But Canada and most of western Europe have their own shortage of IT workers. Some of the original sources of foreign IT workers (Ireland, Israel) have dried up. The main source of H-1B workers is now India. Some people complain about a visa program directed primarily at one country, and about Indian-owned companies in the United States that manipulate the visa system to bring Indian workers as indentured servants to work in consulting firms under subpar conditions. Other countries are now competing with the United States for these foreign IT workers. Early results indicate that green-card programs to attract foreign IT workers are not succeeding in other countries—especially in Germany, where the program is seriously undersubscribed and the foreign workers often feel unwelcome.

Special Issues for the Education Sector

Campus IT staff have been under extreme pressure in recent years as technology changed rapidly, demand increased exponentially, and the lure of quick riches (or even simply a competitive salary) in industry beckoned. These pressures have been addressed in a number of ways that can best be addressed by others, but in the context of a discussion of the supply of IT workers we want to point out a special opportunity and responsibility for the campus IT support organization.

Though already widely used, there may be opportunities in many areas to make better use of students in staffing an IT organization. It takes creative and flexible management and a degree of cooperation between academic departments and support units that too often is missing. The obvious advantages of working at an educational institution (flexibility, good environment, reduced tuition, challenging work, and so on), if properly exploited, can significantly reduce the competitive disadvantage of generally lower salaries and benefits.

At the same time, campus IT support organizations can play a larger and useful role in extending real-world experience to IT students. Again, it takes creative management on both the support and the academic side, but if done well it can be a great boon to academic programs, students, and support organizations alike.

The responsibility (among others) of the educational institution in providing a supply of well-trained and educated IT workers for society is well known, but that is not the subject of this short chapter. An educational institution, especially a large one, is similar to other organizations in needing a variety of IT workers. A special kind of IT worker (the IT-related professor) is desperately needed by many educational institutions at all levels. Without them, there is no supply chain of IT workers.

The proper balance and staffing of the IT-related professorate is a critical issue for campus leaders, but not the focus of this volume. We note, however, the continuing concern of the research community and others that we may be "eating our seed corn" as IT professors are siphoned off into other careers (usually in industry).

Campus IT policies do play a key role, however, in helping attract and retain good educators and researchers—to say nothing of students—in all fields. In IT, these policies and their implementation are critical. Without proper IT systems in place for their education and research programs, IT professors rapidly become frustrated and leave. Most of the research-oriented institutions that we are personally familiar with have solved this problem (at least partially) by dealing with computing support for IT-intensive programs separately from general campus policies. Some aspects of this may always be necessary for good reasons (a computer science professor can't be allowed to experiment with the campus backbone network!), but campus IT policies that do not support IT-related professors are increasingly irrelevant. To end this discussion on a positive note, those responsible for campus IT policies have a special opportunity to help address the issue of producing sufficient IT workers for society.

Women, Minority, and Older Workers

Several groups of Americans are represented in the IT workforce in percentages that are far lower than the percentage in the population as a whole: women, African Americans, Hispanic Americans, and Native Americans. It is probably also true of older workers, but the figures are not available to demonstrate this.

Statistics on participation in higher education in IT-related majors give some indication of the underrepresentation. According to the Department of Commerce, only 1.1 percent of undergraduate women choose an IT-related discipline, compared to 3.3 percent of undergraduate men. Only about 150 African Americans have received doctorates in computer science and engineering in the United States since computing became a recognized academic discipline in the early 1960s. Tables 1.2 and 1.3 show the number and percentage of degrees awarded to women and minorities in the field over time. One of the most depressing observations that can be made from these tables is that the percentage of women receiving degrees has been steadily declining since the mid-1980s. This is in contrast to the progress made in the late 1970s and early 1980s in attracting women to the field. It is also in contrast to the trend in other scientific and engineering disciplines over the past two decades, during which there has generally been an increase in the percentage of women enrolled and graduating.

For purposes of brevity, this discussion is restricted to the issue of women. Many of the same issues discussed later for women apparently apply to underrepresented minorities, but there are also additional issues at play for minorities.

There is not yet hard empirical evidence about why women are underrepresented in this field. The National Science Foundation is funding a number of such studies currently under its IT workforce initiative, and we should begin seeing the first results in the next year or two. However, there has been substantial speculation about this phenomenon. Here are some of the reasons commonly adduced:

- Use of computers in high school (when students are first introduced to them) for playing aggressive and violent games, which turns girls off

- Lack of high school teachers and counselors who can explain the nature of IT education and careers and show the attractions to young women students

Table 1.2. Number of Degrees Awarded in Computer and Information Sciences

Academic Year	Ph.D.'s		M.S. Degrees		B.A. or B.S. Degrees	
	Number Awarded	Percentage Women	Number Awarded	Percentage Women	Number Awarded	Percentage Women
1984–85	248	10.1	7,101	28.7	38,878	36.8
1985–86	344	13.1	8,070	29.9	41,889	35.7
1986–87	374	13.9	8,481	29.4	39,589	34.7
1987–88	428	11.2	9,197	26.9	34,523	32.4
1988–89	551	15.4	9,414	28.0	30,454	30.8
1989–90	627	14.8	9,677	28.1	27,257	29.9
1990–91	676	13.6	9,324	29.6	25,083	29.3
1991–92	772	13.3	9,530	27.8	24,557	28.7
1992–93	805	14.4	10,163	27.1	24,200	28.1
1993–94	810	15.4	10,416	25.8	24,200	28.4
1994–95	884	18.2	10,326	26.1	24,404	28.4
1995–96	867	14.5	10,151	26.7	24,098	27.5
1996–97	857	15.9	10,098	28.2	24,768	27.2
1997–98	858	16.3	11,246	29.0	26,852	26.7

Source: National Center for Education Statistics, 2000.

Table 1.3. Degrees Awarded in Computer Science and Computer Engineering, by Level and Gender

Academic Year	Ph.D.'s		M.S. Degrees		B.A. or B.S. Degrees	
	Number Awarded	Percentage Women	Number Awarded	Percentage Women	Number Awarded	Percentage Women
1984–85	326	11.0				
1985–86	383	13.1				
1986–87	559	9.7				
1987–88	744	9.0				
1988–89	807	13.3				
1989–90	907	12.6				
1990–91	1,074	12.1				
1991–92	1,113	11.3				
1992–93	999	13.6				
1993–94	1,005	15.6	5,179	19.1	8,216	17.9
1994–95	1,006	16.2	4,425	19.7	7,561	18.1
1995–96	906	11.8	4,170	20.4	8,028	16.6
1996–97	892	14.5	4,359	22.7	7,335	17.2
1997–98	933	14.0	4,842	22.6	9,341	16.8
1998–99	852	14.6	5,576	26.3	11,461	17.0
1999–2000	868	15.1	6,181	25.7	13,721	19.2

Source: Computing Research Association, Taulbee Survey, published in Freeman and Aspray, 1999.

- The image of computing as a lifestyle that is not well-rounded or conducive to family life

- Differences in socialization of men and women as to whether they are performing well academically, which may encourage men and discourage women from studying information technology—even when the male and female students are performing equally well academically

- A perception of computing as a solitary occupation, not well integrated into social discourse or social institutions

- A perception that software jobs are not family-friendly (long hours, lack of awareness of the opportunity for telecommuting and other flexible schedules)

- Courses in mathematics and science that are requirements for an IT degree program, which women have not been encouraged to pursue on the basis of outdated stereotypes of aptitude and interest

- The lack of women role models

Although we await the outcome of these empirical studies on the causes, expert groups have made a number of recommendations about how to recruit women and underrepresented minorities into the field (Cuny and Aspray, 2001; Aspray and Bernat, 2000). Some of the recommendations are to give students research experience, establish mentoring programs, make sure there are suitable role models, build a community of underrepresented students so that the students do not feel so isolated, be more accommodating to students who interrupt their academic career or who have a background outside of the current norm, and generally make sure that academic programs are student-friendly.

Conclusion

The United States continues to lead the world in creating new information technology and in finding innovative and productive ways to employ it in all aspects of modern society *because* we have such a broad and deep supply of IT workers. The issues we face today are thus primarily of improvement, not initiation. Within that broad perspective, we believe that this discussion, augmented by the studies in the references, creates a good context for more specific discussion.

References

Aspray, W., and Bernat, A. *Recruitment and Retention of Underrepresented Minority Graduate Students in Computer Science.* Washington, D.C.: Computing Research Association, 2000.

Committee on Workforce Needs in Information Technology. *Building a Workforce for the Information Economy.* Washington, D.C.: National Research Council, 2000.

Cuny, J., and Aspray, W. *Recruitment and Retention of Women Graduate Students in Computer Science and Engineering.* Washington, D.C.: Computing Research Association, 2001.

Denning, P. J. "Computing the Profession." *Educom Review*, Nov. 1998, pp. 26ff. [www.educause.edu/ir/library/html/erm9862.html]

Freeman, P. A., and Aspray, W. *The Supply of Information Technology Workers in the United States.* Washington, D.C.: Computing Research Association, 1999. [www.cra.org/reports/wits/cra.wits.html]

National Center for Education Statistics, *Digest of Statistics*, 2000. [nces.ed.gov/pubs2001/digest]

2

Information Technology Jobs and Skill Standards

Neil Evans

The shift in the United States to an information economy requires a high level of foundation and technical skills in the workforce. Educational and training institutions must restructure themselves to better prepare this new workforce. One effective tool for this restructuring is application of information technology (IT) skill standards.

IT skill standards define the professional job-related knowledge, skills, and abilities required to succeed in the digital-age workplace. They can be used as a foundation tool for developing educational curriculum, profiling jobs, recruiting and evaluating employees, and designing academic and professional certification. They can be used alone or in conjunction with other input, such as that from a subject-matter expert, industry advisory committee, professional organization, existing academic or vendor-specific curriculum, or accrediting organization.

IT skill standards create a common-language framework for educators, industry, and other stakeholders to develop the educational and training tools necessary to prepare students and incumbent workers for today's workplace challenges as well as those that lie ahead. Skill standards can be used for a number of purposes:

- Improving the education and training of the information technology workforce

- Increasing cooperation between education and business

- Improving academic mobility by facilitating development of an articulated curriculum that continues from high school through community or technical college and on to a four-year institution and graduate work

- Establishing criteria and standards for assessment, certification, compliance, and degrees

The National Workforce Center for Emerging Technologies (NWCET), located at Bellevue Community College in Bellevue, Washington, has identified and described skill standards for eight IT career clusters in the publication *Building a Foundation for Tomorrow: Skill Standards for Information Technology.* The millennium edition of this work is the end result of a national review and update of the IT skill standards, with input from expert panels around the country for new and changing skills, work functions, technical knowledge, and related employability skills.

Why Skill Standards?

Most competitive industrialized nations have evolved a well-established professional skill standards system. Applying skill standards to development of curriculum results in courses and programs whose outcomes can be assessed across a range of contextual technical and foundation performance criteria. This results in employees who are prepared to function effectively in the technology- and information-based workplace.

There are numerous benefits to IT skill standards. Companies communicate their performance expectations to their employees, educational institutions reform their curriculum to match workplace needs, and the skills gap between workplace expectation and student preparation can be closed. Among the major stakeholders benefiting from IT skill standards are businesses, IT professionals, students, educators, and government policymakers.

For IT skill standards to be effective, they must reflect the consensus of the industry professionals in the IT career field. To ensure the integrity, quality, and continuity of the skill standards, several principles have guided development:

- Experienced IT workers, who are the experts in their career field, must be used to identify the work performed and the skills, knowledge, and abilities required to be successful.

- Business and education must work together as partners to ensure the link between work expectations and curriculum.

- Skill standards must represent broad career clusters rather than narrowly defined jobs.

- Standards must be flexible and portable and should be updated continually.

- Integrated skill standards must define work duties in the context of the work setting.

Career Clusters

A career cluster is a grouping of representative job titles, related by close association with a common set of technical skills, knowledge, and abilities. The career cluster approach closely reflects how work is organized today, especially in illustrating mobility and progression among representative job titles.

There is a range of IT careers and career progressions within the profession. The IT career clusters identified by NWCET have been broadly adopted by industry, education, and government policymakers as a standard framework for classifying IT jobs and careers

The IT Skills Pyramid

The three-tiered pyramid depicts IT skill standards in three broad IT competency categories: foundation and employability skills, common technical skills, and industry-specific technical skills and organizational knowledge.

Tier 1 is the set of foundation and employability skills, knowledge, and abilities that are required of all information worker employees. These are the universal skills—problem solving, team skills, and flexibility—that are needed to apply technical knowledge and tools effectively.

Tier 2 is the set of technical skills, knowledge, and abilities common to all IT positions within an IT career cluster. For a programmer, for example, knowledge of the principles of programming applies across all industries.

Tier 3 is the set of industry-specific technical skills, knowledge, and abilities that are unique to individual clusters and that are the most susceptible to change. For example, a programmer's required knowledge of data communications and network protocols may differ across companies and industries.

Tier III
Industry-specific
technical skills,
knowledge, and
abilities unique to
individual industries
or organizations

Examples include:
• Knowledge of and compliance with
  company practices and organization
  protocols
• Understanding and effective use of
  industry terminology
• Knowledge of and compliance with
  industry legal requirements
• Knowledge of and compliance
  with company and product standards

Tier II
Technical skills,
knowledge, and abilities

Skills common to all
jobs within a career
cluster across all industries

Examples for IT include:
• Proficient use of software and
  hardware tools
• Proficient use of Internet techniques
• Understanding of
  hardware/system architecture
• Troubleshooting of software and
  hardware problems

Tier I
The set of foundation skills,
knowledge, abilities, and personal
qualities required of all workers to
be successful in today's workplace

Foundation skills
• Basic skills
  (reading, writing,
  arithmetic . . .)
• Thinking skills
• Personal qualities

Workplace competencies
• Management of time
  and resources
• Interpersonal skills
• Management and use
  of information
• Understanding and
  management of systems
• Use of technology

and for quantifying their supply and demand. These are the eight NWCET IT career clusters:

1. Database development and administration

2. Digital media

3. Enterprise systems analysis and integration

4. Network design and administration

5. Programming and software engineering

6. Technical support

7. Technical writing

8. Web development and administration

These career clusters represent a broad range of job titles, from entry level through senior management. They are designed to be usable to educators at every level, and to human resource professionals; training, certification, and assessment developers; students and job seekers; and organizations and individuals conducting research into information technology workforce issues.

Common Elements Across Clusters

Several elements are common across all clusters. This commonality reflects the desire, among virtually all employers, to find employees with a set of common qualities that support specific technical knowledge and skills. These common categories are project management, task management, and problem solving and troubleshooting. Either explicitly or implicitly, certain other process skills appear repeatedly across all eight clusters (analysis, design, development, testing, implementation, and documentation).

The nature of each of these IT skills differs with the job level and from cluster to cluster. By inference, however, employers want employees who can

- Apply a systematic, methodical approach to solving a problem

- Research to see who else knows about the problem

- Develop a rational set of possible solutions

- Test the solutions cost-effectively and efficiently

- Verify that the problem is truly solved

- Document the solution for others

Technical Skills

In addition to these common elements, specific items of technical knowledge, skills, abilities, attributes, and use of tools are associated with a function or task. These are represented at a high level and avoid reference to a specific vendor, version, or piece of equipment. This allows maximum flexibility in adapting the skill standards to local specifications while preserving the employer's general requirements for specific skills.

Employability Skills

Finally, there are employability skills—general requirements associated with a function or task. Input from industry clearly shows that without solid mastery of employability skills, an employee cannot succeed in the highly competitive environment of today's technology company. Employers often say that "technical skills may get you the job, but foundation skills make you a valued employee and significantly increase career advancement." For our purposes, let us identify seven types of employability skills:

- *Communication skills.* Effective information flow throughout the organization is a critical element in organizational success. Communication with team members, supervisors and subordinates, and customers and clients as well as between groups must be timely and appropriate. Some jobs rely heavily on written communication, while others depend primarily on verbal communication. Communication in a high-technology organization takes on many forms: informal or formal presentations, technical logs, complex reports, proposals, and so on. No matter the form, communication is vital to individual and team effectiveness.

• *Organizational skills.* As employees are asked to handle more parallel tasks with an increased level of complexity, good organizational and planning skills become important. Depending on the job, the complexity of the organizational task may vary from scheduling and prioritizing multiple tasks or requests to planning and tracking complex and capital-intensive projects involving many people and teams. Regardless of the size of the project, the ability to identify and define tasks, track milestones, recognize when a project timeline is running into problems, and take appropriate action is crucial to ongoing success in a technical job.

• *Team contribution and leadership.* Most organizations are relying increasingly on teams to accomplish projects. This is particularly true in high-tech environments where the success of a project depends on the contribution of many individuals with varied expertise. The ability to work with team members with diverse backgrounds and communication styles is highly valued and rewarded in most environments. Being able to read the needs of the team as a whole and the needs of individual team members, and to adjust one's role to increase team effectiveness, is essential to the success of the team process.

• *Professionalism.* Dealing with problematic employee issues, attitudes, and behaviors consumes much time in any organization, and it can be quite detrimental to overall morale. Employees with good work ethics, who show up on time, who understand and follow company procedures, and who relate to coworkers and customers with respect are usually the ones selected for a position with an increased level of responsibility and reward.

- *Critical thinking and decision making.* As an organization becomes leaner in management, the employee is expected to assume increased responsibility. An employee's ability to correctly analyze a situation, understand tradeoffs, offer good recommendations, and make the right choice is often rewarded with increased freedom to self-manage, and with the opportunity to engage in more interesting and challenging projects.

- *Customer relations.* Customers can wear many faces. An internal customer is the department down the hall or an offshore division. An external customer is a supplier, client, or end user. The ability to solicit and listen to customer feedback and to effectively address customer issues and concerns is required to qualify for certain positions, such as a technical support job. Customer interaction skills are necessary in every job, whether or not its description formally includes "customer relations."

- *Self-directed and continuous learning.* In the high-technology industry—especially in an information technology environment—technologies and practices change rapidly and sometimes radically. To keep up with technology change, employees must constantly engage in self-assessment against the technological landscape of skills and knowledge and then take proactive steps toward enrolling in continual training for their trade. The employer expects employees to be current in their technical skills. Most organizations provide the necessary resources for continual training. However, it is often seen as the employee's responsibility to identify personal gaps in knowledge and take actions to fill these gaps.

How can one learn employability skills? Most professional or technical and academic programs include some requirement for practicing foundation skills. However, many lack the emphasis that employers would like to see. Being aware of the importance of such skills can help students and employees enroll in a program that emphasizes using, practicing, and coaching foundation skills in the learning process, class activities, and projects. Educators must be aware of the importance of these skills to the long-term success of graduates; they must create ample opportunity for holistic and contextual practice as well as authentic assessment.

Future Trends in IT Skill Standards and Emerging Careers

Some of the trends in an IT career that may be of interest to users of skill standards are e-commerce and e-business, outsourcing, specialization, certification, and nontraditional degree pathways.

E-Business and E-Commerce Careers

E-commerce and *e-business* are often used interchangeably. Arguably, no application of information technology will be more pervasive in the foreseeable future than electronic commerce. Various aspects of electronic commerce affect firms of every type and size, from the home-based proprietor to the global enterprise.

In general terms, electronic commerce is the intensive application of information technology to enable, enhance, and facilitate business transactions. The most obvious examples are consumer-oriented businesses selling directly to end users via the Web. Although these activities have garnered a large share of media attention, the total value of their transactions pales in comparison to business-to-business commercial activity.

E-business is the intersection of Internet technology with critical enterprise applications. Thoughtful application of Internet, intranet, and external technologies either to existing or to reengineered systems can create an electronic continuum of business processes, from marketing promotion to a sales transaction through order processing, logistics, manufacturing, billing, shipping, customer support, and cross-selling. The resulting environment extends significantly beyond a simple commerce phase to create a continuous Internet customer life cycle. The term *e-commerce*, then, is generally limited to using Internet technology in the selling process only.

There are other legitimate interpretations of what distinguishes e-business from e-commerce. One common distinction is that e-commerce describes Internet sales to end users (retail purchases) while e-business defines enterprise-level transactions that may occur between distributors, between business divisions, or between a manufacturer and a vendor, a manufacturer and a distributor, or a supplier and a retailer.

E-commerce will certainly revolutionize how business is done. Entities that may be competitors may find they benefit from "co-opetition"—the coined word describing cooperative competition. The considerations surrounding conduct of business, data integrity, security, rights, access, restrictions, and interoperability are substantial.

IT Outsourcing, Contracting, and Consulting

The trend toward focusing on core business and core competencies that started with large firms is being adopted by smaller firms and educational institutions as well. For information technology, this trend has resulted in an increasing number of long-term contract positions at the technician level and large growth in consulting services at the professional level.

Firms for whom information technology is not a core competency may contract for computing infrastructure, hardware, maintenance, Web site hosting, transaction processing, data warehousing, and employee training in use of technology. This trend has created opportunities for full-time employment with the contractor supplying the service, rather than with the end user of the service. Contract workers often do not have permanent status. Although many assignments extend for the duration of the contract (and are therefore considered long-term), they are temporary because there is no assurance the contract will be renewed or extended. Because of the explosive growth of the information technology industry and the shortage of skilled workers, relatively few proficient individuals have experienced a period of unemployment, and this is expected to be the case for the foreseeable future.

Many firms also employ consultants in short- and long-term positions to help with implementation and integration guidance and to research and offer strategic input (especially in technology forecasting and deployment). Large and small firms also seek consultants with specific skills in current or emergent technologies as they apply to their business needs. A consultant may work independently but is often part of a skilled group whose services are arranged through a large firm specializing in consulting services. People working for these firms often acquire a valuable worldwide enterprise perspective as they work through their assignments, bringing their technical expertise and aggregated experience to each new assignment.

Some educational institutions are also following the IT outsourcing trend, focusing on their core competency (instruction delivery) and their core service (student services delivery). These institutions are usually outsourcing in the areas of internal computing and network infrastructure or Internet access and Web site hosting with Internet service providers (ISPs). Some institutions have even outsourced their entire IT department to a vendor that hires the incumbent IT staff, which allows retention of the staff's knowledge of current operations and business processes. Another emerging outsourcing trend among higher education institutions is contracting out their business or student services application to an applications service provider (ASP).

IT Specialists Versus Generalists

An interesting divergent trend seems to be emerging in the structure of the information technology workforce in large companies as opposed to small ones. Larger firms seem to gravitate toward specialization at both the technical and management levels. Some technical workers support relatively small groups dedicated to one project that is narrow in scope. As a result, there is a tendency to develop extreme experts in a tightly focused area.

Interestingly, educational institutions and some larger companies for which IT is not a core business express strong interest in
finding individuals with a range of skills, knowledge, and abilities.
This implies that the employee is able to determine when the firm
needs to seek external resources and to make the case for justifying
their use when necessary. It also means the employee is more effective when able to communicate not just laterally but to all organizational levels. Since students and recareering adults often start with
small concerns, this trend implies that educational and training
efforts should include activity and assessment that build the student's ability to integrate a range of skills and abilities.

Nontraditional IT Degree Paths and Certifications

The nature of information technology work and the explosive
growth of the field have created opportunities for rapid career progression and salary advancement. The iterative and project-based
nature of the work means an experienced person has increasing
responsibility in project management, planning, and coordination.
There is a trend toward upside-down degrees, where someone at
the technician level acquires additional business education by
which he or she becomes qualified for increasing management
responsibility.

A four-year college, especially one catering to working adults, is
often willing to evaluate technical education and professional development in partial fulfillment of academic degree requirements, and
increasingly willing to offer individualized study and flexible cohort-
based learning groups to facilitate degree completion.

Information technology workers at all levels value their education, strive to stay current, and are often among the employees most
eager to take advantage of professional development and career
advancement opportunities. This trend implies that employers must
continue to offer professional development and career advancement
opportunities; it also suggests that there will be continued growth

in nontraditional undergraduate and graduate education for information technology workers.

Conclusion

IT skill standards constitute a common-language framework for educators, employers, and corporate trainers to develop the educational and training tools necessary to prepare students and incumbent workers for today's workplace challenges. Both IT educators and HR professionals are realizing that these standards can be used effectively as a foundation tool for developing educational curriculum, profiling jobs, recruiting and evaluating employees, and designing academic and professional certification. All major stakeholders in IT workforce development—business, IT professionals, students, educators, government policymakers—benefit from IT skill standards.

Acknowledgments

Much of the content of this chapter, including the figure in the sidebar, is derived from the work of the National Workforce Center for Emerging Technologies (formerly the NorthWest Center for Emerging Technologies), which has been published in *Building a Foundation for Tomorrow: Skill Standards for Information Technology—Millennium Edition*. Copyright 1999 NorthWest Center for Emerging Technologies and Bellevue Community College. All rights reserved. Sponsored in part by the National Science Foundation through grant number DUE 9813446.

3

IT Fluency
What Is It, and Why Do We Need It?

Herbert S. Lin

Why do we need to know about information technology? Surrounded by computers, electronic communications, digital information, and software, many of us are coming to realize that a better understanding of information technology is valuable in our work and personal lives. This realization is based on a number of factors:

- Information technology has entered our lives over a relatively brief period of time with little warning and essentially no formal educational preparation for most people.

- Many who currently use information technology have only a limited understanding of the tools they use and a (probably correct) belief that they are underutilizing them.

- Many citizens do not feel confident or in control when confronted by information technology, and they would like to be more certain of themselves.

- There have been impressive claims for the potential benefits of information technology, and many would like to realize those benefits.

- There is concern on the part of some citizens that changes implied by information technology embody potential risks to social values, freedoms or economic interests, etc., obligating them to become informed. [National Research Council, 1999, p. 1]

These factors raise a concern: What should everyone know about information technology to use it effectively now and in the future? To answer this question, the Computer Science and Telecommunications Board (CSTB) of the National Research Council initiated a study in August 1997. Although the study group was initially formed as the Committee on Information Technology Literacy, its members quickly decided that literacy was too modest a goal. Computer literacy has acquired a "skills" connotation, implying competency with a few of today's computer applications, such as word processing and e-mail. As the technology relentlessly changes, existing skills fall out of date and there is no migration path to new skills. Indeed, the computer is just over fifty years old, the personal computer is less than twenty years old, and the World Wide Web has been widely known for less than five years. In the face of such rapid change, a better solution than having a repertoire of skills is for an individual to be able to adapt to changes in the technology. One might ask, What should the class of 1946 have been taught about information technology?

Though skills are surely necessary, no fixed set of skills suffices. In addition to skills, people must gain a sufficient foundation to be able to acquire new skills independently after completing their formal education. Hence the CSTB study committee adopted the term *fluency* and titled its final report *Being Fluent in Information Technology* (National Research Council, 1999). In a briefing for the committee, Yasmin Kafai noted that "fluency connotes the ability to reformulate knowledge, to express oneself creatively and appropriately, and to produce and generate information (rather than simply to comprehend it)" (National Research Council, 1999, p. viii). Fluency with information technology (what the committee's report calls "FITness") "entails a process of lifelong learning in which individuals continually apply what they know to adapt to change and acquire more knowledge to be more effective at applying information technology to their work and personal lives" (p. 2).

One way to understand the limitations of a traditional computer-literacy approach is to draw an analogy that compares a native resident of a city to a person who has visited the city several times. Consider how each person might drive from the airport to some final destination. The visitor's understanding of the local geography is limited; he or she has probably learned one route that worked well in the past. On the other hand, the resident has a fuller (more fluent) knowledge of many streets and landmarks. Thus the visitor is prone to wait out a traffic jam, while the resident is more likely to find an alternative route because of his or her broader understanding of landmarks and arterial streets. Similarly, a computer-literate person who has only basic information technology skills, such as word processing, e-mail, and Web browsing, may be unable to adapt to solve a problem not previously encountered.

What Is IT Fluency?

The study committee determined that fluency with information technology requires three kinds of knowledge: contemporary IT skills, foundational IT concepts, and intellectual capabilities. Exhibit 3.1 lists the ten highest-priority items for these three types of knowledge, each of which prepares a person in different ways for FITness.

- *Contemporary skills*, the ability to use today's computer applications, enable people to apply information technology immediately. In the present labor market, skills are an essential component of job readiness. Most important, skills provide a store of practical experience on which to build new competence.

Exhibit 3.1. Knowledge Required for FITness

Intellectual Capabilities
1. Engage in sustained reasoning
2. Manage complexity
3. Test a solution
4. Manage problems in faulty solutions
5. Organize and navigate information structures and evaluate information
6. Collaborate
7. Communicate to other audiences
8. Expect the unexpected
9. Anticipate changing technologies
10. Think about information technology abstractly

Information Technology Concepts
1. Computers
2. Information systems
3. Networks
4. Digital representation of information
5. Information organization
6. Modeling and abstraction
7. Algorithmic thinking and programming
8. Universality
9. Limitations of information technology
10. Societal impact of information and information technology

Information Technology Skills
1. Setting up a personal computer
2. Using basic operating system features
3. Using a word processor to create a text document
4. Using a graphics and/or artwork package to create illustrations, slides, or other image-based expressions of ideas
5. Connecting a computer to a network
6. Using the Internet to find information and resources
7. Using a computer to communicate with others
8. Using a spreadsheet to model simple processes or financial tables
9. Using a database system to set up and access useful information
10. Using instructional materials to learn how to use new applications or features

Source: National Research Council, 1999. Copyright 1999 National Academy of Sciences. Reprinted with permission.

- *Foundational concepts*, the basic principles and ideas of computers, networks, and information, underpin the technology. Concepts explain the how and why of information technology, and they give insight into its opportunities and limitations. Concepts are the raw material for understanding new information technology as it evolves.

- *Intellectual capabilities*, the ability to apply information technology in complex and sustained situations, encapsulate higher-level thinking in the context of information technology. Capabilities empower people to manipulate the medium to their advantage and to handle unintended and unexpected problems when they arise. The intellectual capabilities foster more abstract thinking about information and its manipulation. [National Research Council, 1999, pp. 2–3]

The skills, linked closely to today's computer usage, change over time, but the concepts and capabilities are timeless. These three types of knowledge occupy separate dimensions, implying that a particular activity involving information technology involves elements of each type of knowledge. Although learning the skills and concepts and developing the intellectual capabilities can be undertaken independently, such an approach does not promote FITness to any significant degree. Each of the three elements of FITness is essential, and each is equal to and reinforces the others.

FITness Is Personal, Graduated, and Dynamic

The study committee determined that FITness is personal in the sense that individuals fluent with information technology "evaluate, distinguish, learn, and use new information technology as appropriate to their own personal and professional activities. What is appropriate for an individual depends on the particular applications, activities, and opportunities for being FIT that are associated with the individual's area of interest or specialization" (p. 3).

One of the earliest points at which people come to understand the personal nature of FITness is when they first encounter what might be called the "magical instructor effect." This is often displayed in the presence of students; it goes something like this. The instructor gives students an exercise to perform on the computer. A student raises his or her hand to say, "I need help, because I did what you said and nothing happened." When the instructor walks over and tells the student to do it again, the student does so, and lo and behold, as if by magic, the right thing happens. The student then says, "But I just did the same thing a minute ago, and it didn't work for me!"

Of course, the source of the magical instructor effect is that the proximity and hence oversight of the instructor prompt the student to work more carefully. The second time—in the instructor's presence—the student does indeed follow the directions properly, whereas in the first instance, he or she did something that was approximately but not exactly the same thing. Because computers are quite sensitive to the difference between approximately-the-right-thing and exactly-the-right-thing, failure ensues the first time but not the second.

The magical instructor effect is relevant for two reasons. The first is that, for most people, it clearly demonstrates the unforgiving and relatively brittle nature of information technology compared to the relatively forgiving and flexible responses of human beings. The second is that the presence of the instructor can force a student to recognize that information technology is used in a context—and in this case, the context is highly personal.

The committee found that FITness is graduated in the sense that it is characterized by levels of sophistication (rather than a single judgment of fluent or not fluent), and it is dynamic in that it entails lifelong learning as information technology evolves. Thus they recommended that "FITness should not be regarded as an end state that is independent of domain, but rather as something that develops over a lifetime in particular domains of interest and that has a different character and tone depending on which domains are involved" (p. 3).

The Role of Colleges and Universities in Promoting FITness

The study committee suggested that colleges and universities are an important community in which to promote FITness. One key reason is that K–12 teachers are themselves taught in colleges and universities. Because what happens in K–12 education is so dependent on what K–12 teachers know and feel comfortable with, promoting FITness in colleges and universities has important effects on the effort to promote such fluency among K–12 students.

A college or university also has an important role in promoting equity. Individuals with few opportunities, resources, wealth, or access to public facilities are often disenfranchised by technological advances. To promote a goal of all students graduating FIT, a college or university may need to make a concerted effort to help such individuals overcome their lack of exposure and preparation in this area.

Finally, the committee felt that it may be easier to promote FITness in colleges and universities at first, compared to K–12 schools or noneducational settings. One reason is that a college or university generally enjoys greater autonomy in changing curricula, as compared to a K–12 school (or school district). Second, it tends to have more computing infrastructure than a K–12 school and is better able to invest in technology infrastructure.

It is undeniably true that an increasing number of students are entering college with important information technology skills. Many now know how to use a word processor, e-mail, a Web browser, and how to download music files. But as already described, skills are not sufficient. Moreover, the context in which the student has developed these skills is not necessarily one that promotes acquisition of foundational concepts or broad intellectual capabilities. It is for this reason that project-based learning offers such promise.

A Project-Based Approach Is Best

Although Exhibit 3.1 presents the content of FITness as a list of items, such a characterization does not imply that lecturing about them is the optimal form of instruction. FITness is fundamentally integrative, requiring coordination of information and skills with respect to multiple dimensions of a problem and the need for making overall judgments and decisions taking all such information into account.

Thus the study committee recommended a project-based approach "to weave together the skills, concepts, and capabilities of FITness to achieve a tangible result" (p. 54). Working on a project, students use and become skillful with specific information technologies such as database, e-mail, and presentation software. As they begin to understand the range of alternatives and implement the solution, they rely on and become motivated to learn the underlying concepts.

An appropriately scoped project demands collaborative effort. According to the study committee, project-based collaborative effort is pedagogically valuable for several reasons:

- First, developing true expertise in any area requires the individual involved to assume a variety of different roles—creator, critic, partner, supporter, and so on—and a collaborative group effort is a natural setting in which to exercise these roles. Furthermore, learning to specialize and to deliver one's special information to a group is an important dimension of developing expertise, and so project-based learning helps teach students the character and nature of varied roles as well as how to play the role of a specialist.

- Second, a project requiring multiple collaborators can be large and complex enough to raise important intellectual and strategic issues that simply do not arise when problems are artificially delimited to be completely doable by a single individual.

- Third, students benefit from hearing explanations formulated by peers as well as experts. [National Research Council, 1999, p. 54]

The Core Curriculum Concept

In the project context, it is helpful to address a concept not unfamiliar to colleges and universities: a core curriculum. The metaphor of a core curriculum is in fact quite powerful; it is worthwhile to extend it beyond conventional usage, drawing on an analogy developed by Philip Morrison (1964).

Consider the core of an apple. It has all of what one needs to grow apple trees. If one's goal were to see apple trees all over the country, shipping apple cores to every state would seem quite efficient; they are compact, light, easily shipped, and require no refrigeration. So what would happen if the nation tried to grow apple trees this way?

The net result of this approach would be very few apple trees. Why? Because it takes a lot of work to nurture an apple tree from a core. The seeds have to be planted, and watered at regular intervals. Appropriate soil must be found. Crows must be chased away and prevented from eating the seeds. If people didn't know how apples taste, and simply relied on a cookbook in which apples are listed as an ingredient, who would be willing to do all that work? Some might, but most would not; hence only a few trees would be planted and take root and give fruit.

It is for this reason that context matters. Only by understanding the context of personal value and use can one appreciate why learning something is important. In the culinary context, value comes from knowing how apples taste. In the FITness context, value comes from knowing how fluency with IT is put to use in a personally meaningful endeavor—and that comes from the project-based approach to learning already described.

The study committee concluded that "successful implementation of FITness instruction will require serious rethinking of the college and university curriculum. It will not be sufficient for individual instructors to revisit their course content or approach. Rather, entire departments must examine the question of the extent to which their students will graduate FIT. Colleges and universities will need to concern themselves with the FITness of students who cross discipline boundaries and with the extent to which each discipline is meeting the goals of universal FITness" (p. 5).

One approach to FITness across the curriculum is a single course, open to all students. In such a course, students complete a series of projects that facilitate their acquiring FITness capabilities while developing their understanding of the concepts and skills of FITness. For example, one such course developed by the chair of the study committee included a project called "Truth or Fiction," which called for students to make up a bogus Web site. The point of the assignment was to emphasize that you can't believe everything you read on the Web and to understand both how to give credibility to a site and how to recognize misinformation. (Faking a photo with Photoshop was part of the task; it produced some impressive results!)

Of course, in the usually packed undergraduate curriculum, adding one course means taking away another—something that most institutions are loathe to do. An alternative approach to adding a single course draws on the idea that information technology is pervasive and that, when properly integrated, fluency in IT—as with the ability to write well—benefits the study of any subject. With this approach, eventually faculty in many subject areas incorporate the concepts, skills, and capabilities of FITness into the context of problems drawn from their own field. George Mason University has adopted a variation on this approach; see Chapter Six for a discussion of lessons learned from implementing GMU's Technology Across the Curriculum program.

Conclusion

In summary, the study committee concluded that "FIT individuals— those who know a starter set of IT skills, who understand the basic concepts on which IT is founded, and who have engaged in the higher-level thinking embodied in the intellectual capabilities— should use information technology confidently, should come to work ready to learn new business systems quickly and use them effectively, should be able to apply IT to personally relevant problems, and should be able to adapt to the inevitable change as IT evolves over their lifetime. To be FIT is to possess knowledge essential to using information technology now and in the future" (p. 5).

Acknowledgments

This chapter is based on the findings of the Committee for Information Technology Literacy, which were published in the report *Being Fluent with Information Technology* (Washington, D.C.: National Academy Press, 1999). The author was study director for the project that resulted in this report. Copyright 1999 National Academy of Sciences. Reprinted with permission.

References

Morrison, P. "Less May Be More." *American Journal of Physics*, 1964, *32*(6), 441–457.

National Research Council, Committee on Information Technology Literacy. *Being Fluent with Information Technology*. Washington, D.C.: National Academy Press, 1999. [books.nap.edu/books/030906399X/html/index.html]

Part II

Campus Challenges and Solutions

4

Campus Human Resource Leadership
A Mandate for Change

Lauren A. Turner, Susan Perry

Although higher education institutions are often stereotyped as change-resistant, technology-driven change on campus is as pervasive as it has been in the general workforce and society at large. Technology, however, is not the only catalyst for change. Global and domestic competition for students, budget pressures, the decreasing ability of prospective students to pay ever-increasing educational costs, evolving expectations of what it means to provide a high-quality education, and the exploding potential for innovation in teaching and learning have presented a set of nearly unimaginable challenges to the higher education enterprise. It is, in fact, technology that often allows higher education to respond effectively to these other changing needs.

Campus human resource (HR) professionals are as pivotal to their institution's establishing an effective response to such change as are information technology (IT) professionals. Historically, however, many campus HR departments have not been regarded as partners or players in institutional strategic planning. On the contrary, HR staff have been regarded as paper-pushers and gatekeepers, the people who make sure that employees are put on the payroll and enrolled in benefits and that policies and procedures are followed. This history has not facilitated—in fact, it has impeded—the kind of engagement that is essential to help guide institutional response to the many challenges created by the technology revolution.

Today, on many campuses the role of the HR professional has evolved so that he or she is expected to work as a peer with other senior campus administrators in developing institutional strategic plans, in recognition of the larger potential value he or she can add (Connolly, 1999). The HR professional is knowledgeable about the business of higher education and of the role technology plays in it, is strong in the functional areas of managing people, and is competent in establishing and maintaining credibility with all campus constituent groups by facilitating and practicing effective working relationships. In establishing this new role, HR professionals have begun to change many of their longstanding practices and policies so that they are more fully integrated with the goals and challenges now facing their institution.

In this chapter, we address the human resource challenges that are presented by the reality that, in our current work environment, technology touches every employee and every student in some way or other. We recommend strategies that your institution can consider in responding to these challenges, emphasizing the importance of a partnership between HR and IT.

Human Resources: Leading and Supporting Change

Over the last decade, jobs have changed as rapidly and unpredictably as the weather. Customer demands for services and employer expectations of the employee's contribution to meet those demands have increased in parallel. Correspondingly, the level of required job skills and performance expectation has risen sharply.

The availability and application of new technologies is one of the primary drivers of this change and is now, more than ever before, a basic cost of doing business. Some other factors that have affected the pace of change are the increase in the number of women and people of color entering the workforce, competition to include nontraditional modes of educational delivery, and the growth and development of a global economy.

A clear business case for change exists. Successful colleges and universities are committed to finding ways to keep pace with technology change; in this regard, they recognize the growing importance of the role of human resources as an agent of continual transformation (Ulrich, 1998). An institution's technology strategy clearly must be an enterprisewide initiative and embody the principal goals and objectives of the institution. In academe, there is always a potential for both support for and resistance to any change initiative. Success is often a result of a consultative process that involves the members of the community who have a stake in and commitment to the outcomes; the HR leader is in an excellent position to help facilitate that consultative process.

To remain viable and competitive, a college or university knows it must create and maintain academic and administrative systems that keep pace with technological change and, most important, support the mission and key institutional goals and objectives. These systems form the infrastructure to support institutional success, but they also pose significant challenges.

Support for Transforming Teaching and Learning

The potential for using IT to support teaching and learning is exploding. Application of technology in the curriculum presents many challenges as the higher education institution attempts to effect change in traditional methods of educating. The institution must critically evaluate academic programs, even to disassemble and recreate them so as to position itself and the faculty to effectively integrate technology into teaching and learning.

To support this transformation, the campus must employ a sufficient number of staff who have the necessary competencies to facilitate this process of change and innovation with integration of technology into the educational mission. These competencies include not only technical skills but also the interpersonal and communication skills to effectively negotiate relationships with faculty and other more computer-savvy customers, including staff and students.

Support for Administrative Change

A college or university is also pressed to put in place effective and efficient administrative systems. Clunky, slow, inefficient, centralized, administrative systems driven by the Computer Center are a thing of the past. Slick, fast, efficient, decentralized, user-driven administrative systems have taken their place. They require a significant increase, though, in the technology knowledge base of the front-line user. They also require central information technology support staff to develop new competencies to communicate, plan, and support these end users.

An institution simply cannot follow through on changing administrative systems strategies without a concerted HR effort to ensure that the right personnel are hired and retained—not just IT personnel, but personnel throughout the institution. The IT skills of these new employees need to be state-of-the-art and their communications skills fluent.

The HR-IT Partnership

A partnership between an institution's chief human resource officer (CHRO) and its chief information officer (CIO) can greatly facilitate proactive planning for and garnering of institutional, employee, and community support as well as implementing campus initiatives in response to technological change.

The combined expertise and campus clout of the CHRO and the CIO are important. Each administrator brings to the table his or her relevant functional expertise. The CIO brings the knowledge of technology and pertinent market information about technology change trends, as well as operational understanding of the business of the division. The CHRO brings knowledge of human resource management, including recruitment, compensation, legal considerations, employee relations, a campuswide perspective on these issues, and the relevant market information about trends in the business of human resources.

The success of the partnership between these administrators depends on the effective command of their respective expertise. It also depends on their ability and willingness to trust each other and work toward common institutional goals, on their comprehensive understanding of the business of higher education and their institution specifically, and on their ability to establish and maintain working relationships with many constituencies at all levels across the institution to promote credibility and trust in their work and expertise.

In some institutions, this partnership may come naturally. However, in an institution with a history of adversity in the relationship between HR and other departments as a result of its administration of policies and practices, it takes more work to develop the relationship. A positive working relationship can develop out of an adverse situation, but this happens only if both parties are willing to listen to each other, trust in the expertise that each brings to the table, and acknowledge the institutional goals that are important for them to achieve together. Learning from each other's expertise and perspective (asking "What are your concerns?"), sharing information that supports a position or opinion, and being willing to "move your stake" facilitates this partnership.

IT is everywhere, and colleges and universities are vulnerable to the market. To be successful in the face of such vulnerability, HR and IT partners must identify the challenges and work together toward an agreed-upon solution. Human resource practices have to be moved out of their black box. For example, sharing salary survey data and discussing benchmarking strategies builds credibility and a shared ownership of the outcomes; HR gains comprehensive understanding of IT vulnerability and challenge, and IT gains better understanding and respect for internal equity issues. The result is tremendous synergy and a credible, productive partnership that can influence and inform campus strategy.

Technology Everywhere: Changes and Challenges

Integrating technology into work processes has resulted in a significant shift as to where and how work is accomplished, and in many cases as to who is responsible for actually doing the work. The consequence of this integration of technology is that almost every person on campus is exposed to technology in his or her work, studies, or basic campus communications.

Most employees now need to be proficient in technology to some degree if they are to be successful in their jobs. This phenomenon has resulted in a blurring of the line of functional responsibility between traditional IT workers and other campus employees.

In addition, management of information through technology is increasingly decentralized, with employees across the institution engaged in technology-based work. Some of this decentralization of IT work has resulted in establishing technically oriented positions in various functional areas. It has also resulted in the significant evolution of many jobs across campus that now entail technology components ranging from use of spreadsheet, database, and word processing programs and data analysis tools to establishment and maintenance of Web pages, as well as increased involvement and accountability in selecting and maintaining administrative computing systems.

In this "technology everywhere" environment, job descriptions are changing incessantly—new jobs are emerging, not only in IT departments but in all departments, creating expectations for job reclassification both for IT workers and IT-enabled workers. With change in classification, expectations arise for commensurate change in compensation systems.

Earlier classification and compensation systems designed by many HR departments across industries, with the help of consultants, did not take into consideration the kind of skill and competency essential to accomplish today's work or to compete for talent in today's workforce. These were often point-factor systems that rigidly and somewhat arbitrarily assigned values to skills, experience, and education and left little or no room for flexibility. A college degree was often required if a position were to be rated as professional-level, and promotional increase was limited to 5 percent or minimum of the new salary grade. Furthermore, salary grade was established by benchmarking only with other institutions of higher education.

Such rigid and narrowly focused criteria often resulted in conflict between HR and hiring departments because employees were unhappy with their compensation level and potential for position and salary advancement, hire-in salary range was not competitive enough to recruit the talent needed, and the systems were holding back elevation of positions as a result of antiquated rating and factor designations.

Recruitment practices were also in need of retooling. As the job market shifted and the skill levels required of prospective employees increased, colleges and universities were slow to expand their recruitment horizon beyond the higher education market. This phenomenon was especially true in hiring administrative office and IT professionals, where there was significant competition for applicants with strong technology skills.

Strategies for Dealing with Change

Which strategies have helped to meet these challenges? What can your campus do to ensure that human resource issues receive the attention they demand? One exemplary plan has been articulated by the University of California system, as part of a "new business architecture" developed to "manage growth, control costs, improve the work environment, and implement best business practices" (New Business Architecture Planning Group, 2001, p. iii). As one of six key components of the architecture, the people section of the UC plan suggests a set of simple but powerful strategies for leveraging human resources in the digital age (Exhibit 4.1).

From our experience at Mount Holyoke College (see the sidebar for our case study), we have found similar strategies to be successful,

Exhibit 4.1. People Strategies

Improve Recruitment and Retention
- Promote the institution as an employer of choice
- Streamline the hiring process
- Expand outreach to increase diversity
- Create flexible benefits
- Improve job design and classification
- Institute market-competitive compensation

Improve Professional Development and Productivity Strategies
- Customize training approaches, including an on-line training and development curriculum to complement and enhance current training offerings
- Expand training and development programs for core competencies in supervision/management, interpersonal skills, and basic technology
- Expand and build upon professional development offerings in leadership and other professional skills for career mobility (classes, internships, fellowships, other experiential learning)
- Create and build upon training programs and internships for employees to become information technology professionals (for example, an in-house "IT University")
- Deploy additional staff resources when required by significant growth or new requirements
- Develop new on-site and off-site initiatives to deepen skills in managing complexity
- Strengthen orientation and acculturation initiatives to build community
- Improve workforce planning, including labor-management partnerships

Source: New Business Architecture Planning Group, 2001, p. 17. Copyright 2001 The Regents of the University of California. Reprinted with permission.

beginning with making the people challenges strategic and being a proactive part of process and organizational change. Both human resource and information technology leaders must gain support from senior management to move discussion about human resources and technology to a more central and strategic place in campus planning. Technology planning can no longer be a peripheral or stand-alone activity; it must be incorporated into the institutional planning and strategic direction-setting process.

The CHRO, CIO, and their staff can bring their respective expertise to a partnership that results in identifying and implementing creative strategies for supporting technology growth with limited human resources and for leveraging the power of "technology everywhere" to benefit the institution in many ways.

Distributing IT Skills and Talent

Working together, IT and HR staff can establish a group of employees from across campus to function as a network of local experts who partner with IT staff in all kinds of activity to support the growing demand for technology development, education, and training.

HR can play a leadership role by proactively capturing information about the skills and capabilities of employees throughout the institution so that their talent can be leveraged in deploying them on various project teams as needed. This has been described as a "knowledge management" role for HR (Roberts-Witt, 2001). Since such teams must be formed and reformed rapidly to adapt to changing campus requirements, HR managers have to become proficient at mobilizing and dismantling project teams (Boyett, Boyett, Henson, and Spirgi-Hebert, 2001). The University of Minnesota is in the process of adopting such a skills-inventory approach, identifying which skills exist in the institution to benchmark and train against and to be used to inform the hiring process. The aim is to hire people who can be mobile within the university, with more general skills, so that they can be moved around the organization as needed for special projects.

As a result of this strategy of deploying staff as needed to work on critical projects, employees who would not ordinarily be involved in a campus initiative beyond their own position and limited departmental role have the opportunity to be involved on a team to work on a project with campuswide impact. A college or university is a relatively flat organization with limited opportunity for career development inherent in its structure. This leveraging of employee technology skills opens up prospects for really garnering the talent of existing staff to meet important institutional goals.

HR and IT need to work together with academic and administrative department heads to identify the local experts and gain departmental support for the concept. Local experts can serve in a train-the-trainers capacity in their department; act as liaison between

---

Mount Holyoke College: A Case Study in Organizational Change

Mount Holyoke College (MHC) is a private, liberal arts college for women, located in western Massachusetts. It has two thousand full-time undergraduate students and one thousand employees. Like our peer institutions, Mount Holyoke has had its share of change initiatives resulting from technology. We have learned a lot along the way about which approaches to implementing change have worked and which have not. One of the key things we have learned is how much our organizational culture (which strongly promotes interdepartmental communication and collaboration) and our organizational structures are tremendously valuable in successfully implementing change initiatives.

Becoming a High-Performance Organization

In the early 1990s, Mount Holyoke's senior management, under the leadership of the president and in coordination with the human resource department, embarked on a strategic initiative to become a

IT and the department; help identify, test, and prioritize new technologies and their uses; and even identify office ergonomic concerns.

A potential concern about such an approach might be that the staff who are identified and invited to participate must be fairly compensated for the more advanced technology role they are assuming. We address this concern in discussing salary administration programs.

Providing Technology Training for Everyone

Recognizing that many campus employees are struggling to learn new technologies, HR must implement strategies to help current employees develop their skills. An important philosophy of any technology training initiative is development of employee self-sufficiency in using the technology. Although support from a help

---

high-performing, inclusive organization. Two key elements to reaching this goal are having a defined mission and vision—with identified institutional strategic initiatives to serve the mission and vision—and having an infrastructure to support this work. A major component of this infrastructure is norms on how people in the organization are expected to interact.

As a result of this work, for more than a decade MHC's management teams have worked in an environment that calls for communication, partnership, collaboration, and respect for and value of individual contribution. Managers are expected to understand the mission and priorities of the college and to keep the business of their departments in alignment with these goals. They are further expected to encourage interdepartmental and intradepartmental teamwork.

Restructuring the Library and IT Organizations

Approximately six years ago, under the leadership of the provost, MHC's computing, library, and electronic services departments

desk and ongoing training opportunities are important, a key goal should be to develop technology skills throughout the institution.

It is important to recognize that adult learning styles vary, and that this demands a flexible approach to training opportunities. Traditional classroom training, although more expensive and time-intensive than other alternatives, can be an effective approach to teaching some employees. Collaboration with other institutions or departmental trainers (again, the train-the-trainer approach) can be a useful alternative for employees who need this hands-on guidance and support. A self-paced training program on CD-ROM or an e-learning course allows an employee to go to a computer laboratory, take the program back to the office, or carry on the training from home.

---

underwent restructuring that involved merging these previously separate entities into one organization, Library, Information and Technology Services (LITS). This restructuring resulted in some initial anxiety from both employees of the merging departments and campus users of library and technology services. Employees asked, What do books have to do with technology? Why is administrative computing a part of this merger? What is the college trying to accomplish by the merger? How will the merger affect me and how I do my work? Faculty and administrative departments questioned: What's going to happen to services? Will my needs be met? How will the integration of library and IT services be better? What will this change mean to me and my job?

The chief human resource officer and the chief information officer worked closely in planning for and implementing this restructuring from the onset. Six years later, we can say with confidence that the goals of the merger were achieved. We have successfully integrated the three organizations. The effective partnership between HR and IT was a key success factor.

Training and retraining of IT staff (addressed in more detail in Chapter Five) is also an important component of rethinking from a human resource perspective. Higher education has significant IT needs; however, they are relatively stable and do not generate the same potential for regular exposure to exciting new technologies as is true in the more dynamic dot-com world. As we mention later, the potential for stability can be valuable, but it can also be regarded as fatal by the IT professional looking for growth potential.

Every college and university must find a way to offer the opportunity for skills development for IT staff. There is no downside to keeping employee skills fresh. Although helping employees develop their IT skills also increases their marketability, supporting employees in maintaining state-of-the-art skills serves the institution well.

Benefits of the Reorganization

There have been many advantages to this integration in both the academic and administrative realms of information technology. Faculty have seen increased outreach by members of LITS. We have developed the position of instructional technologist in the LITS organization, dedicated to support of faculty in integrating technology into teaching and learning.

The instructional technologists work closely with the librarians who have themselves significantly integrated technology into their teaching and research instruction activities. This role requires LITS staff to command communication skills and scholarly experience and, in turn, creates credibility for them with faculty and students. This allows them to effectively aid faculty in identifying ways information and technology can be integrated into their courses and to enable them to effectively guide and support faculty and students in the use of information and technology in teaching and learning. In many ways, LITS staff are functioning as change agents and change facilitators.

Employees are exposed to new technologies for which they can imagine use on their campus, and such training promotes positive morale by letting the employees know that their contribution to the institution, as well as to themselves, is valued.

Identifying Core Technology Competencies

The ability to use technology is an essential competency for success in just about every job on campus, especially office jobs. It is important to develop strategies to expand the competency level of current staff, but it is also important to recognize the occasion of a vacancy for HR and IT to work together to establish a set of core technology competencies for new office hires.

Here are suggested prerequisite skills for all new office and administrative hires:

This structure has also facilitated the establishment of campuswide teams to evaluate technology trends and advances in support of administrative and academic pursuits, including campus networking, the implementation of a new financial accounting system, a courseware management system, mediated classrooms and training facilities, and most recently, the establishment of a student information systems review team.

Also as a part of this restructuring, LITS was able to gain institutional commitment to establishing adequate budget reserves to fund computing equipment upgrades, to secure a commitment to an increased dedicated commitment of staff to the quality and quantity of our Web presence, and to building our campus networking resources and capabilities.

- Basic word processing

- Basic spreadsheet familiarity

- Use of a Web browser

- Basic printer and file sharing

- Use of e-mail

- File management

- Basic hardware use and maintenance

- Appreciation of work analysis and work restructuring

Although the labor market has seen many shifts over the last decade in terms of the quantity and caliber of available workers, campuses have seen a recent and significant increase in the technical skill and experience in the administrative support applicant pool. As a result, they have been more successful in recruiting new office professionals who have well-developed fundamental technology skills.

Many current employees are motivated by the skill changes expected of them. Still, it is not uncommon to encounter incumbent staff who are unable to develop these core technology competencies because of resistance or inability; consequently, the campus must have a strategy to deal with this. Although it is important to recognize and make time to support development of these employees, unfortunately the end result may be termination of the employee. This can be difficult for the institution, the employee, and the employee's peers, especially if the employee has a record of previously successful service to the institution. The decision must be made thoughtfully and implemented carefully. Alternatives can be considered, such as another job opportunity that does not require the same level of technical skill or the incentive of early retirement.

Creating Flexible Salary and Classification Systems

The technology revolution requires an institution to retool its salary and position classification systems to include job factors that appropriately recognize and value the changing role of technology in campus jobs. A job evaluation instrument used to collect information about position duties, responsibility, experience, and education may need redesigning to collect better information about the tech-

---

Flexible Salary and Classification Systems

A number of higher education institutions have restructured job design and compensation systems to accommodate changing skills requirements in the digital age, especially within the information technology community.

One of the first to tackle this challenge, in the early 1990s, was the California State University (CSU) system, which implemented a six-classification series for IT that aggregated work functions on the basis of common outcomes and skills (core functions) (Swan and Giunta, 1994). The accompanying change in the compensation system involved the negotiation and implementation of broad bands and skill levels for more than one thousand union employees, a process that took more than three years (Giunta, 1997). Virginia Commonwealth University adopted CSU's successful model in 1996, expanding on the use of competencies by relating them directly to the performance management and pay-for-performance process (Benenson-Farley, Hall, and Giunta, 1997).

Another early initiator of major change in this area was the University of Michigan, which in 1996 implemented MSCALES, a three-tiered compensation strategy that converted 140 position classifications to five functionally defined broad bands and reformed the compensation system "to place value on the skills and competencies exhibited by

nical competencies of a position since technology competency is now a part of most jobs on campus.

The institution must redefine the criteria and competencies by which a job is classified in order to recognize the changing nature of the job and create a more flexible compensation system that acknowledges the diverse skills and responsibility inherent in a job. To be viable, the new system also requires close linkage with market salary data that cross industries and are not specific just to higher education.

---

the staff in the achievement of business successes" in the IT division (Tibbs, Pryor, and Smallegan, 1997).

State-supported public universities can face special challenges because of outdated and rigid civil service compensation plans and lengthy and bureaucratic hiring processes. When it became nearly impossible to recruit and retain IT professionals in the mid-1990s, the University of Wisconsin and other Wisconsin state agencies brought their plight to the attention of the state's Department of Employment Relations, which responded by creating the Information Technology Compensation Advisory Council. After studying the problems with the existing IT classification and compensation system, the council recommended creation of a broadbanding system that placed "equal value on the actual job and experience and qualifications of the person," a dramatic departure from "traditional thinking in state government, which places value almost exclusively on the job rather than the person" (Duwe and Caruso, 1998, p. 30).

More recently, Duke University undertook an IT staff broadbanding initiative that established a technical career path for IT staff and created a flexible and competitive compensation program. Sixteen salary grades were replaced by six broad career bands, and ninety job titles were reduced to fifteen to emphasize common core competencies (Dronsfield, 2000).

Another successful strategy is developing a salary-grade structure that uses a broadband approach. Such a structure permits a high degree of flexibility to set salary within a broader range, and more ability to recognize individual skills, experience, and value of the contribution to the institution. Further, in actually assigning a position to a grade, an effective salary administration system must consider not only the data collected from internal assessment of the position but also market salary information. This process can be challenging; the goal is to find a constructive balance between internal equity and market competitiveness. (See the sidebar for a description of several universities that have implemented a flexible classification and compensation system for IT professionals.)

Once a salary administration system has been redesigned, it must be reviewed regularly. Historically, systems have been set in place and left to become antiquated. A dynamic and effective salary system is only maintained if it is proactively administered. Periodic review of positions, regular assessment of market shifts, monitoring of turnover trends, and ongoing benchmarking of salary grades and position levels are essential in maintaining a viable salary administration and position classification system.

Rethinking Other HR Practices

Even after modifying a compensation system to permit flexibility and to appropriately value skills and experience, the institution might still be unable to offer the top salaries that some other industries pay. Thus the HR department also has to rethink its recruiting and retention strategy, including award systems.

Higher education can market its benefits packages and the quality and richness of the work environment as part of the recruiting process. Stability, challenging and complex work, a collegial environment, a healthy balance between work and life, and the potential for a contribution to be recognized and valued are all pluses in the higher education environment.

A good HR organization also reevaluates alternative reward systems so that it can retain valuable staff, especially during a period when the market is competitive for those employees. Market surges or special campus needs always necessitate institutional response to minimize loss of valuable employees throughout the institution. Among alternative reward programs: a lump-sum bonus or other award to recognize accomplishment on a particular project, a bonus to be paid at a future date to entice staff to stay through a crunch period and possibly beyond (a staying bonus), a merit-type pay system that recognizes differing levels of contribution, and other types of in-kind reward such as a gift certificate or time off.

Conclusion

The kind of transformation required for your institution to survive and thrive in the technology revolution requires enterprisewide commitment to and support of information technology goals. Forging a partnership between HR and IT is pivotal to success. The influence and credibility of the partnership can heighten awareness of the value of IT, facilitating a campus commitment of resources and responsiveness to internal and external drivers of change and identifying areas of vulnerability.

There are many creative strategies for meeting people challenges in the digital age. We recommend these:

- Making the people challenges strategic and a proactive part of process and organizational change

- Remaining attentive to the work environment and employee expectations

- Establishing a campuswide commitment to good people management that ensures competitive salaries and benefits, promotes fair and equitable treatment, recognizes individual and team contributions, and creates opportunities for professional development

- Distributing IT skills and talent, which entails capturing information about campus employee skills and capabilities so that talent can be leveraged by deploying people on a project team as needed

- Identifying core competencies and offering technology training for everyone

- Creating flexible salary administration and position classification systems

- Rethinking HR practices to attract and retain the most outstanding employees in a competitive market

Your campus HR and IT leaders can encourage an effective response to "technology everywhere" by monitoring and understanding the trends and applying them intelligently and responsibly. This collaborative approach to planning can prepare your institution to respond to changing needs quickly and effectively.

References

Benenson-Farley, M., Hall, M., and Giunta, C. "Partnerships: New Approaches to Compensation Management for Information Technology Professionals." In *Broadening Our Horizons: Information, Services, and Technology— Proceedings of the 1996 CAUSE Annual Conference.* Boulder, Colo.: CAUSE, 1997, pp. 2-2-1+. [www.educause.edu/ir/library/text/ CNC9610.txt]

Boyett, J. H., Boyett, J. T., Henson, R., and Spirgi-Hebert, H. *HR in the New Economy: Trends and Leading Practices in Human Resources Management.* PeopleSoft, 2001.

Connolly, T. R. "Transforming Human Resources in Higher Education." In D. Oblinger and R. Katz (eds.), *Renewing Administration: Preparing Colleges and Universities for the 21st Century.* Bolton, Mass.: Anker, 1999.

Dronsfield, A. "Duke University's IT Staff Broadbanding Initiative." *EDUCAUSE Quarterly*, 2000, *23*(1), 6–15. [www.educause.edu/ir/library/pdf/eq/a001/eqm001.pdf]

Duwe, J., and Caruso, J. "IT Salaries: Wisconsin Partners to Compete." *CAUSE/EFFECT*, 1998, *21*(4), 30–31. [www.educause.edu/ir/library/html/cem9846.html]

Giunta, C. "New Approaches for Compensating the Information Technology Knowledge Worker." *CAUSE/EFFECT*, Summer 1997, pp. 8–16. [www.educause.edu/ir/library/html/cem9723.html]

New Business Architecture Planning Group. *UC 2010: A New Business Architecture*. Oakland: University of California, 2001. [uc2010.ucsd.edu]

Roberts-Witt, S. L. "Reinventing HR." *Knowledge Management Magazine*, Sept. 2001. [www.destinationcrm.com/km/dcrm_km_article.asp?id=958]

Swan, E., and Giunta, C. "Organizational Effectiveness and Changing Job Design in the Information Technology Community." *CAUSE/EFFECT*, Summer 1994. [www.educause.edu/ir/library/text/cem9426.txt]

Tibbs, J., Pryor, T., and Smallegan, P. "MSCALES: A Broadbanding Approach for Information Technology Professionals." In *Broadening Our Horizons: Information, Services, and Technology—Proceedings of the 1996 CAUSE Annual Conference*. Boulder, Colo.: CAUSE, 1997, pp. 6-3-1+. [www.educause.edu/ir/library/text/CNC9643.txt]

Ulrich, D. "A New Mandate for Human Resources." *Harvard Business Review*, 1998, *76*(1), 124–134.

5

Recruiting, Retaining, and Reskilling Campus IT Professionals

Allison F. Dolan

What a difference a few months can make! In September 2000, 76 percent of respondents to a *CIO* magazine survey reported that information technology (IT) workers were hard to find; in May 2001, just 20 percent gave the same response.

Because of the fluctuations in the IT job market, it is generally imprudent to follow the current fad or get caught up in media hype. There are, however, a set of strategies and principles related to recruiting and retaining staff that, if implemented, improve the chances of success in a tight labor market as well as in times of high unemployment. These strategies may be used in a mix-and-match fashion. Think of the whole landscape as a jigsaw puzzle. All of the pieces do not instantaneously fall into place; progress is made by joining one or two pieces together at a time and positioning them in roughly the right area of the puzzle. Over time, more pieces link together until you have the final coherent whole.

Whether in higher education or industry, the mechanics of recruiting, retaining, and reskilling IT staff are similar, even though the context differs. In fact, there is much that campus administrators can learn from their corporate counterparts about these activities. Thus the guidelines offered in this chapter draw on experience and recent research from the academic and corporate worlds.

Partnering with HR

Imagine an ideal world. Each institution of higher education has a central human resource (HR) organization staffed with certified HR generalists and specialists who view their mission as working collaboratively with the schools and departments to achieve the mission of the institution.

The HR staff is not only aware of what is going on elsewhere in higher education but is active in the HR profession, perhaps as members of the Society for Human Resource Management (SHRM) or the College and University Professional Association for Human Resources (CUPA-HR). The research and best-practice white papers from such organizations are routinely reviewed and appropriately incorporated into the institution's HR strategies. Legal risks associated with hiring and employment practices are minimized.

Industry salary surveys are regularly monitored and recommendations initiated regarding market equity increases. There is a recruiting staff that knows how to effectively attract candidates, backed up by an engaging job Web site and a sophisticated yet easy-to-use applicant-tracking system. High-quality, diverse résumés show up daily, and the typical search is closed within a matter of weeks.

The campus HR department creates a job classification system that balances structure and flexibility, so as to be responsive to changing job requirements as well as changing salary expectations. Compensation is not limited to base pay but includes forms of variable pay (technology bonuses, short-term pay increases). In short, HR is responsible for the infrastructure services needed to manage people in the same way that the IT organization is the steward for the technical infrastructure for the school.

An HR department that performs this way benefits the entire institution, not just the IT department(s). In many cases, campus IT organizations have forced attention on their staffing issues because of the media attention paid to dot coms and the impact of technology in the workforce. In some cases, IT departments have felt compelled to take matters into their own hands, creating their own internal HR function. This may be a matter of necessity in the short run, but in the long run the partnership between the chief information officer (CIO) and the chief human resources officer (CHRO) discussed in the previous chapter is preferred. Even if a strong partnership does not exist at the senior level, progress can be made if IT and HR managers work together.

Recruiting

Higher education IT workers are drawn from the same pool of candidates as financial institutions, retail stores, and manufacturing firms use. To be a player in attracting high-quality candidates, a college or university must use the same sort of recruiting techniques employed by industry. It might be argued that many of the difficulties campuses have experienced in competing with industry have more to do with the lack of recruiting expertise than with lower salaries and lack of stock options.

Best practices for recruiting typically start with some form of focused effort, most frequently housed in the HR organization. Such a function has stewardship of the overall recruiting process, though it is not necessarily responsible for performing all the interviewing and selection. The strategies outlined in this section are best carried out in the context of such a focused recruiting effort. Contrast this with a campus where IT hiring is handled in the IT department by the same manager who is trying to install an enterprise administrative system or Web-based learning application on schedule and on budget. Rather than spend the time needed to do recruiting, the beleaguered IT manager hunkers down and gets the technical work done, leaving the staffing problems to fill infrequent lulls in "real" work.

A good example of a creative and effective recruiting effort in higher education is Wisconsin's establishment of a state-level IT recruiting function. Over the past few years, the chief information officers of the state government and the University of Wisconsin have partnered with the State Department of Employment Relations on a number of initiatives aimed at improving the recruitment and retention of IT staff. Three years ago, the CIOs pooled their funds and hired a state IT recruiter to lead their recruitment efforts. This individual, who is dedicated full time to recruitment efforts, is able to constantly seek creative methods to promote state IT jobs and effect "a solid link between the IT managers and human resource professionals" in the state system (Caruso and Gebert, 2000).

A skilled recruiting function can help the hiring manager create the job definition, identify critical skills and behavioral competencies, write and place the job advertisements, prescreen candidates, schedule interviews, train the interviewing team, answer candidate questions, handle reference checks, and even coordinate the job offer. The ideal recruiter has a good base of general HR knowledge so that she or he can help the hiring manager avoid legal land mines during the recruiting process. Having a defined and disciplined process reduces the risk of a claim of unfair hiring practices.

Developing a Brand

Every sustainable recruiting program begins with a clear understanding of why people are interested in working for a particular institution. Also known as developing a "brand," this is the first step in the marketing program that is the essence of successful recruiting.

Your institution may already have a defined brand for attracting students; if so, it is a good starting point for defining the brand for attracting staff. In addition, you can ask new hires what factors appealed to them, and ask long-time employees what motivates them to stay. Some attributes you might hear:

- Appeal of the higher education mission (especially compared to companies that are forever trying to satisfy Wall Street investors)

- Workplace flexibility (variable work hours, tele-commuting options)

- Access to personal development (63 percent of visitors to the techies.com Web site said the opportunity to learn new skills is very important in evaluating an employer)

- Job stability (at least compared to a start-up company!)

- Good benefits

Some characteristics that may appeal especially to IT professionals:

- Fewer work hours (the average IT professional works more than forty-five hours per week)

- Less pressure (a higher education environment is typically less intense than, say, the IT shop at a major airline or an on-line retailer, where even a few minutes of downtime can result in major losses)

- "Extreme casual" dress (jeans, T-shirts); although many companies allow "business casual" dress, only 27 percent condone extreme casual

- Access to "toys"—the latest and greatest laptops, PDAs (personal digital assistants), and so forth

- Heterogeneous technical environment

Despite the impression created by the media during 1999 and 2000, not every IT professional worked in a dot-com company. Nor do most IT professionals work in high-tech firms. According to the Information Technology Association of America (2001), non-IT companies employ ten times as many tech workers as do IT companies.

Once you know what attracts people to your specific institution, the recruiting staff can focus the advertising in ways that attract desirable candidates.

Sourcing Candidates

In Chapter One, William Aspray and Peter Freeman discuss the supply side of the IT worker equation, noting in particular that the vast majority of IT workers do not have a degree in an IT-related discipline. This suggests that a campus starting its job advertising with "Required: B.S. in computer science" is disadvantaging the search from the beginning.

Employee referrals are a powerful source of candidates for a variety of positions, including IT (Neely, 2001). Many organizations have found that a referral bonus of $100 to $1,500 can stimulate staff to think about people they know who might be a good fit. Referral programs are well researched, and a variety of aids exist to help an organization implement a program; they have been found to be one of the most cost-effective recruitment tools.

Boomerang employees are those who left a while back and are now interested in returning. Some progressive organizations deliberately stay in touch with former employees, continuing to include them in e-mail lists or inviting them in for events. When there is a job opening, the former employee is contacted to see if he or she is interested. Even if uninterested in returning (yet), the person may know a colleague elsewhere who is interested.

A placement agency is also an alternative to, or adjunct to, campus recruiting staff. An agency can be used from the beginning of the search, or used as a last resort if internal efforts have not yielded results. Having a central HR function that can qualify and coordinate relationships with a small number of preferred companies is highly desirable.

Contracting is a well recognized form of staff augmentation. A contract company, especially a larger one, has a well-developed recruiting and screening process. It can often handle a range of staffing needs, from contractors through temp-to-perm.

Chapter One also addresses H-1B issues. For some institutions, it may not be politically or administratively feasible to consider H-1B. For those that can, the October 2000 changes in H-1B policy offer some advantages to higher education ("Universities Would Gain . . . ," 2000). Although it is totally inappropriate to think of foreign nationals as a pool of cheap labor, the reality is that they may be willing to accept positions at the lower end of the market pay range. A campus with student or faculty diversity goals may find this path to increasing staff diversity appealing.

A later section of this chapter about reskilling discusses developing existing campus staff, or offering internships to students or others. All of these represent potential internal sources for IT staff, as do your institution's own graduates who have IT interests and skills.

Recruiting Tools

Many organizations are shifting most of their job advertising from expensive, low-exposure print media (which can cost from $3,000–7,000 for a one-time ad in a major metropolitan newspaper) to lower-cost, wider-distribution Internet job boards ($200–400 for thirty to sixty days).

According to a recent survey, 78 percent of respondents felt their recruiting dollars were best spent using Internet job postings, with only 12 percent saying the same about print classifieds ("Facts and Figures," 2001). Monster.com continues to attract the highest percentage of the job-hunting traffic; dice.com and techies.com are sites that specialize in IT staff.

Although free job boards can sound appealing, unless there is reason to believe that desirable candidates frequent those sites the time and effort to post there may not be worth it. A focused recruiting function can track the effectiveness of various forms and venues for job postings and negotiate the most favorable pricing on behalf of the institution.

In addition to posting positions on commercial job boards, some effort should be made to point job seekers to a job Web site for your campus. Attributes of an effective site include having a job site reference on the home page and an easy way for job seekers to submit applications. Job sites at Microsoft and Compaq Computer have been mentioned as good examples.

There are other techniques, such as hosting or attending a job fair and building a relationship with community career centers, which an appropriately resourced recruiting team can leverage on behalf of the organization.

Logistics of Managing the Applicant Pool

The good news about Internet job sites such as Monster.com is that a hiring manager typically gets dozens if not hundreds of résumés. The bad news is that a hiring manager gets dozens if not hundreds of unqualified résumés. If the applicant system at your campus is still largely geared to paper submission, you should seriously consider an overhaul of the applicant-tracking infrastructure.

There are a number of software tools available to help an organization manage résumés. Professional HR organizations do periodic technical reviews of tools and publish their findings.

Because of the IT underpinnings of any solution in this space, implementing a new applicant tracking infrastructure is a unique reciprocal working opportunity. HR can use IT help with the technology, which in turn enables the IT organization to attract and hire the staff needed to assist departments such as HR.

Conducting Interviews

If your institution has a clear brand that is effectively used in your job advertising, then those who apply have a propensity for finding your environment attractive, even if the money isn't as much as they could get elsewhere. There are excellent sources of information (for example, Rosse and Levin, 1997; Camp, Vielhaber, and Simonetti,

2001) that can be shared with hiring managers to help elevate the hiring and interviewing process to a strategic level, tying hires at all levels to your institution's mission.

Because interviewing is one key to a successful hire, this process should not be left to chance. Here again, HR can play a major role, with general instructions or (preferably) just-in-time interviewing training for the hiring manager as well as any others involved. (Having team members—and even customers—involved in the interviewing increases the probability that a hiring decision will be a good one.)

HR can coach the hiring managers not to be overly focused on technical skills but instead to also explore whether the candidate has the particular behavioral competencies needed for success at your institution. Typical competencies in an IT world are ability to learn, customer orientation, and problem solving. (See the discussion of other such skills and competencies in Chapter Two.)

The HR department can also help a hiring manager weigh the various technical skills. Certainly the candidate needs to be at least technically acceptable; however, expecting a 100 percent perfect match is not necessarily ideal. Some hiring professionals advocate the 80 percent rule for hires: accept less than an 80 percent match and the person is likely to be overwhelmed by the new job; look for significantly more than that and the job may not be sufficiently challenging to sustain their interest.

It is equally important to understand an individual's motivational fit—the specific reasons the candidate is interested in a specific job. No matter how perfectly the technical skills fit, a department should avoid a hire whose personal values, interests, and motivational needs are not aligned with what the organization can offer.

Retaining the Staff You Want to Retain

A successful retention program starts with the recruiting process, carries through the first few weeks of employment, and permeates the work environment all year long. Some elements of it, such as good benefits and compensation in line with market, typically require HR approval and implementation. Other (often more important) aspects such as creating a sense of affiliation, alignment with the departmental mission, and opportunities for development, are primarily the responsibility of the hiring department staff (Eleey and Oppenheim, 1999). A positive work environment not only lowers attrition, which reduces the need to replace staff; it also creates positive buzz about an organization, making it easier to recruit and retain staff.

Retention starts with asking people why they stay. In describing retention research done by the Gallup organization, Marcus Buchingham and Curt Coffman (1999, p. 28) identified twelve questions that correlate very strongly with retaining the staff one wants to retain. Among those questions were the following:

- Do I know what is expected of me at work?
- In the last seven days, have I received recognition or praise for doing good work?
- Is there someone at work who encourages my development?
- Are my coworkers committed to doing quality work?

It is worth noting that "pay" is not even mentioned in any of the twelve questions.

Salary

When it comes to retaining IT staff in higher education, salary is typically mentioned as a problem. Not only have many campuses been structurally limited because of prevailing job classification and salary structures, but they have also struggled to understand how they can pay their IT professionals more than they are paying faculty and other academic staff who are, after all, the reason the IT staff is needed in the first place.

Although in study after study salary is not typically one of the top five retention issues, it does become a major issue if people perceive they are seriously underpaid, individually or collectively. Compensation professionals tend to consider organizational average salaries that are within 3–5 percent of the market to be close enough.

In reviewing several salary surveys that categorize results by industry, "education" often falls 8–10 percent below the overall average. Some surveys (such as the Hewitt HOT Technologies IT salary survey; see www.compensationcenter.com) calculate a tenth and twenty-fifth percentile. Senior management may decide that all acceptably performing staff should be paid at least at the tenth percentile. (Salary survey information such as this can also be incorporated into establishing the minimum pay for IT salary bands.) In one recent survey, the tenth percentile was on average 22 percent below the median pay.

In addition to base salary, your institution may want to consider other compensation options, such as a retention bonus (to retain someone with valuable traditional IT skills), a technology bonus (to recognize an individual with currently hot skills or critical legacy system knowledge who may not warrant a large base-salary increase), a performance bonus (to recognize significant efforts that exceed the norm), or a milestone bonus (often offered as an incentive to complete a phase of a project by a specific date).

There are many sources for credible IT compensation information, among them the Mercer IT Compensation Survey (www.imercer.com), Ivy Plus Compensation Survey (www.wmgnet.com), the Hay Local Area Pay Survey (www.haygroup.com), the Hewitt HOT Technologies Survey referred to earlier, and the salary.com Web site (www.salary.com). The HR department in a college or university should use a mix of higher education and industry surveys to set the best context for decisions regarding salary and other compensation.

Reward and Recognition

Showing appreciation for effort is a highly important element of retention. Many organizations have a formal reward and recognition program. Awards do not need to be large to be meaningful. A $50 gift certificate, delivered in a timely way with sincere words of appreciation, can mean as much as (or more than) several hundred dollars showing up in a paycheck six months later without explanation.

Staff Development

Some organizations shy away from investment in staff development for fear that newly trained staff will then leave. However, considerable research indicates that an organization's commitment to staff development is linked not only to productivity improvement but also to increased staff loyalty (*2001 ASTD State of the Industry Report*, 2001).

Employee development is so much more than classroom or online training. The most effective and valued development comes in the workplace, facilitated by mentoring and coaching from supervisors, followed up with projects and activities that allow an individual to experiment and exercise new skills. Given how quickly training can atrophy, application of new skills is critical to success. In addition, development must be recognized as an unending set of activities, not one or two training events.

Leadership Development

There is a wealth of recent literature to support the thesis that retention correlates to relationships between managers and staff (Bernthal and Wellins, 2000; Buchingham and Coffman, 1999; Joinson, 2001; O'Reilly and Pfeffer, 2000; West, 1998). Although a departing staff member may say she is leaving because of the money, it is often true that the employee is receptive to another offer because the supervisor hasn't communicated the organization's goals and directions, provided individual performance feedback, acknowledged work that is done well, created opportunity for development, or otherwise engendered personal loyalty.

Technical team leaders may not recognize their role in retention. Selecting the right competencies for a leadership role and working with leaders improves the quality of the work output, of course, and it is also a vital element of retention.

Reskilling

There are at least two categories of reskilling: developing non-IT candidates into IT staff, and developing new skills within existing IT staff.

Reskilling IT Staff

Unlike some professions that require long years of study, in IT many skills can be developed relatively quickly—over a period of weeks or months instead of years. Unfortunately, not a lot of research exists about how long it takes to develop an employable level of proficiency, so IT managers need to rely on their own experience (or anecdotal evidence) in other organizations. For example, in the early days of Windows NT, a proficient VMS systems administrator could competently manage an NT server essentially immediately. In general, a good Unix system administrator can add another Unix variant to his or her portfolio in less than six months, and it takes a good applications developer about the same time to begin getting results with a new language or new developer toolkit.

As part of the planning for reskilling, the manager responsible for the reskilling must address the following issues:

- Assessment of which skills the organization needs

- Assessment of the individual's current skills (technical and nontechnical), the gap relative to the desired state, and the probability that the individual can achieve the

desired skills on the basis of demonstrated ability
to learn

- Who will be doing the training, coaching, or
mentoring

- How much reskilling is formal classroom training as
opposed to other techniques such as on-line training,
self-study, and so forth

- How the individual undergoing training will gain the
necessary practical experience in a timely way

For most organizations, the issues related to the training itself
are often overshadowed by the problem of release time for the individual. All too often, an employee is expected to learn the new
skills while continuing to support a portfolio of systems or customers. If at all possible, arrange to release individuals from a majority of the old work so they can focus on the new. (The fact that
people are often reluctant to let go of the familiar can be an equally
challenging effort!)

Turning Non-IT Workers into IT Staff

A number of programs have been developed at colleges and universities to offer IT training to non-IT workers. In an *EDUCAUSE
Review* article, Brian Alexander and Kent Kuo (2001) described the
FastTrack program implemented at the University of California,
Davis, which established a focused internship program for a small
number of students, with the goal of having ready-to-hire staff by
the time the students graduated.

Another example is Purdue University's award-winning Information Systems and Technology Training Program, designed to
address the university's need for IT professionals by creating a new
applicant pool from within the university and without. After successfully completing the training, internally sponsored applicants

return to their sponsoring department, ready to accept new responsibilities requiring IT skills (Yuochunas, 1998).

Still another example is Alamo Community College's intern program, which gives a career development opportunity to an individual with a minimum of a two-year degree and no computer training who wants to train to be an analyst/programmer (Burmeister and Martinez, 1998).

A program that simultaneously employs and educates students in information technology is the award-winning Student Technology Services (STS) program at the University of Wisconsin, Milwaukee. A work-based learning organization, STS employs about three hundred students to deliver technology services to the UWM campus in more than twenty functional areas. It is entirely managed by students, with a unique organization structure and professional development program in which the students are the decision makers, budget and program managers, service providers, and technology paraprofessionals. More than half of STS participants are from nontechnology academic programs. Full-time IT staff serve as mentors to student supervisors, and a partner program with the local business community gives students external workplace experience and helps to develop a pool of future employees (see www.uwm.edu/IMT/STS for more details).

Such programs, which offer developmental opportunities to students or other institution staff, have several advantages, not the least of which is an existing sense of affiliation (which is an element of retention). Although some students can't wait until they leave campus, others are more than willing to remain in an environment they know and are comfortable with.

Competency Modeling Related to Development

Whether you are reskilling IT staff or bringing in non-IT candidates, it is important to understand that some competencies are easier to develop than others. For example, if someone lacks the ability to learn (that is, attends classes but doesn't seem able to put the training into practice), it is almost impossible to modify that particular competency. On the other hand, a competency such as strategic thinking can be developed. Competencies that are difficult to develop include taking initiative, decision making, and flexibility. Screening candidates for the reskilling program for these competencies significantly improves the chances for success.

Conclusion

For various reasons, many institutions of higher education have lost touch with the research and best practices associated with recruiting and retention that are widely reported in HR journals as well as IT trade magazines and business publications. Although some recruiting and retention tactics such as stock options may be unique to private enterprise, the strategies and principles explored in this chapter are equally effective in an institution of higher education. Evaluating your institution's current practices with regard to recruiting, retention, and reskilling of IT professionals—as well as the relationship between your HR and IT organizations, especially at the leadership level—is an effort that could pay big dividends.

References

Alexander, B., and Kuo, K. "IT Staffing on the Fast Track." *EDUCAUSE Review*, July–Aug. 2001, pp. 14–15. [www.educause.edu/ir/library/pdf/ERM0148.pdf]

Bernthal, P. R., and Wellins, R. S. "Retaining Talent: A Benchmarking Study." Development Dimensions International (DDI) Web site, 2000. [www.ddiworld.com/pdf/cpgn60.pdf. 2000]

Buchingham, M., and Coffman, C. *First Break All the Rules: What the World's Greatest Managers Do Differently.* New York: Simon & Schuster, 1999.

Burmeister, C. W., and Martinez, E. A. "Overcoming the IT Staff Crisis at Alamo Community College District." *CAUSE/EFFECT*, 1998, *21*(4), 23–24. [www.educause.edu/ir/library/html/cem9846.html]

Camp, R., Vielhaber, M. E., and Simonetti, J. L. *Strategic Interviewing: How to Hire Good People.* San Francisco: Jossey-Bass, 2001.

Caruso, J., and Gebert, J. "IT Recruiting: Great Candidates Can Be Found." Paper presented at EDUCAUSE 2000 in Nashville, Tenn., Oct. 2000. [www.educause.edu/ir/library/pdf/EDU0034.pdf]

Eleey, M., and Oppenheim, L. "Retaining IT Staff Through Effective Institutional Planning and Management." CAUSE/EFFECT, 1999, 22(4), 17–25. [www.educause.edu/ir/library/]

"Facts and Figures." Human Resource Executive, Oct. 1, 2001, p. 86.

Information Technology Association of America. 2001 Workforce. Washington, D.C.: Information Technology Association of America, 2001. [www.itaa.org/workforce/studies/hw00execsumm.htm]

Joinson, C. "Employee, Sculpt Thyself, with a Little Help." HR Magazine, May 2001, pp. 61–64.

Neely, M. "The Headhunter Within, Turn Your Employees into Recruiters with a High-Impact Referral Program." HR Magazine, Aug. 2001, pp. 48–55.

O'Reilly, C.A., III, and Pfeffer, J. Hidden Value: How Great Companies Achieve Extraordinary Results with Ordinary People. Boston: Harvard Business School Press, 2000.

Rosse, J. G., and Levin, R. A. High-Impact Hiring: A Comprehensive Guide to Performance-Based Hiring. San Francisco: Jossey-Bass, 1997.

2001 ASTD State of the Industry Report. Alexandria, Va.: American Society for Training and Development, 2001.

"Universities Would Gain from New Senate Immigration Bill." Washington Update, Mar. 13, 2000. [listserv.educause.edu/archives/update.html]

West, A. "The Information Technology Staff Crisis: Plan for It!" CAUSE/EFFECT, 1998, 21(4), 13–18. [www.educause.edu/ir/library/html/cem9844.html]

Yuochunas, N. L. "Purdue University's IST Training Program." CAUSE/EFFECT, 1998, 21(4), 28–29. [www.educause.edu/ir/library/html/cem9846.html]

6

Technology Across the Curriculum
Information Literacy and IT Fluency

Anne Scrivener Agee, John G. Zenelis

If information technology skills are increasingly important in the world outside of higher education, then certainly educators need to examine the programs of study at their institution to see how they are preparing students to survive and thrive in the technology-rich environment that has now permeated all areas of life.

Information literacy, fluency in information technology (IT), technology across the curriculum, general education requirements, ubiquitous computing—there are many models for introducing technology into academic programs, but no silver bullet that meets the needs of every institution. We are not attempting here to define one approach that every institution should take. Instead, we focus on factors that every institution needs to consider in successful curriculum development for fluency in information technology and information literacy, and we offer examples of strategies that can address these factors. Although we present these factors linearly, they are really recursive—consideration of any one factor may lead back to reconsideration of others.

In addition, although we focus here on curriculum development for undergraduate education, we recognize that the strategies we identify also have broader application to the design of continuing training programs for workforce development at the college or university level or in the work setting. The growing industry of IT-related training needs to be cognizant of the same range of factors as academic institutions in order to create successful programs. Supplying information technology workers and IT-enabled workers is a task that higher education shares with employers, and both sectors need carefully planned strategies to be effective in meeting that responsibility.

In our discussion, we have used examples from George Mason University's Technology Across the Curriculum (TAC) initiative because we are most familiar with it, but we would be the first to acknowledge that George Mason's program was designed to fit this institution's particular circumstances and is not necessarily appropriate at another institution. (Specific information about the TAC program is available on the Web at cas.gmu.edu/tac/.)

Preliminary Definitions

Information literacy and information technology fluency are overlapping but distinct competencies. They are complementary to each other—in today's world an information technology fluent person must also be information literate, and vice versa. In this context, the aim of *fluency* in information technology tends to focus on the technology itself; the goal of *literacy* is primarily concerned with the intellectual framework of dealing with information. Both competencies, however, require development of a continuum of evolving skills that become possible through mastery of interrelated concepts and cultivation of broad intellectual capabilities.

In Part One of this book, Herbert Lin gives an overview of what IT fluency consists of and comments upon its critical importance, drawing on the findings of a National Research Council study (1999). Mastery of the three types of knowledge (contemporary skills, foundational concepts, and intellectual capabilities) characterizes fluency in information technology, or FITness. These are the essential building blocks for acquiring knowledge of and sustaining the process of lifelong learning for FITness, bolstering a person's ability to succeed in the dynamic environment of information technology. Although the concept of FITness clearly goes well beyond the mechanical type of learning typically associated with computer literacy (some might label it vocational training), its focus nevertheless remains information technology itself—hardware, software, networks, and so forth.

In contrast, the central concern of information literacy "is an intellectual framework for understanding, finding, evaluating, and using information—activities which may be accomplished in part by fluency with information technology, in part by sound investigative methods, but most important, through critical discernment and reasoning" (Association of College and Research Libraries, 2000, pp. 3–4). Development of information literacy focuses on information itself:

- Determining the nature and extent of information needed

- Finding and accessing needed information effectively and efficiently, whether it is available in the library, on the Web, from a government agency, in a book or journal, or in a map

- Critically evaluating information and its sources and using it effectively

- Understanding the ethical, legal, economic, and social uses of information

Like FITness, information literacy aims to develop, foster, and sustain lifelong learning. But unlike FITness, information literacy abilities are not exclusively or ultimately intertwined with or dependent on information technology.

Ten Keys to a Successful Program

In thinking about how to integrate either or both of the related concepts of IT fluency and information literacy into the curricula of an institution, we have identified ten factors as crucial elements in a successful program.

Determine Your Institutional Stakeholders

An environmental scan is an important early step in addressing technology in the curriculum. Who cares, or might potentially care, about this issue? The list is certain to vary from institution to institution, but here are a few suggestions:

- Does your governing board take a strong interest in curriculum?

- Has your regional accrediting agency or state higher education board set guidelines for technology or information literacy competencies?

- Has the business community in your area expressed a need for employees with technology skills?

- Do some academic departments already offer technology-related courses?

- Are there faculty committees involved in curriculum development?

- How important is it to your students to develop their technology and information literacy skills?

- How do your alumni feel about an effort to include more technology skills in your institution's degree programs?

Don't overlook in your environmental scan academic support units such as the library, student services, and information technology—and even the public relations department, the development office, and institutional research staff. The staff in these units are very likely to have not only an interest in the issue but the expertise to contribute to developing a successful initiative.

Any or all of these groups can be a tremendous ally in developing a unified and coherent institutional approach to improving student technology and information literacy skills. Conversely, they can also be a tremendous roadblock if they feel that their perspectives or interests in the issue are not being addressed by the proposed program. At the very least, your program will be deprived of their potential contributions of time, funding, or expertise if the program coordinators are unaware of their interest in the issue.

For George Mason's program, the governor and the state legislature (with their concern for workforce development) turned out to be key players in initiating TAC. But the actual design and implementation required many participants within the institution.

Not every group of stakeholders has the same strategic importance, of course, but institutional change being as difficult as it is, one supporter more or one resister less can make a difference in the success of the overall program.

Engage Your Stakeholders

Having identified stakeholders or potential stakeholders in the issue of student technology and information literacy skills and their respective levels of strategic importance, you need to engage them appropriately.

At a minimum, you can engage stakeholders by sharing information through a Web site, brochure, e-mail announcement, and the like. At a higher level of engagement, you can actively solicit input on the project through a survey or focus group. For example, in designing TAC, faculty were surveyed quite early in the process to find out the degree to which they were already asking students to use technology in their courses and what kinds of technology they were using. By being able to give a big-picture view of what was already happening, we could show that our proposal aligned with a direction in which faculty were already moving.

We used focus groups both with faculty and members of our local business community to get ideas about exactly what technology skills students needed to succeed in an academic discipline and in a business environment. The high degree of overlap between the two groups helped faculty recognize that TAC had academic value and was not a vocational sellout to nonacademic concerns.

Other levels of active engagement include membership on a working group or project team, a proposal review board, and an advisory group. Whatever you can do to translate interest to participation and ultimately into ownership benefits the program. If it is seen as (or, in fact, is) the work of only one or two people, it is much more difficult for the program to have long-term staying power, impact, and acceptance.

The TAC program also uses showcases to continue engaging stakeholders. At our annual celebration of student learning, for example, TAC sponsors a prize for the learning project that demonstrates the best incorporation of technology in learning. We also have a prize sponsored by the university libraries for the best original student research to encourage development of information literacy skills. Hundreds of students and faculty visit the event and are impressed with what their colleagues are learning and doing with technology.

Define Your Terms

Now, with all these interested parties engaged in your program, there are a lot of ideas floating around about what the program should be. Multiple perspectives and a multitude of ideas can be healthy and helpful at some stages of development, but eventually the participants have to come to consensus on what the program really is and what they are actually buying into.

What would technology integrated into the curriculum look like at your institution? Does it mean every student takes a technology course? That every faculty member uses technology in delivering instruction? That every course requires students to use technology to complete the learning? That some courses or some students or some faculty use technology—and if so, which ones?

Perhaps more basically, what does "technology" encompass? Are you focusing on office applications such as word processing and spreadsheets? Do you also include on-line search and research skills, information literacy skills broadly defined, multimedia skills? What about legal and ethical issues related to technology, such as privacy, security, and copyright? Do you include use of such technology equipment as digital cameras and data projectors, computer operating systems, and programming languages?

None of these possible definitions is necessarily the best for every type of institution. There can be excellent reasons for including or excluding certain features from your institutional approach. But to make the program work, everyone needs to know what is included and what is excluded so that the participants' energy is focused on the former. The strategies of engagement already mentioned also facilitate definition of terms and buy-in on the program definition.

One cornerstone of TAC is a list of ten technology goals. It took almost a year of collaboration to come up with this list, but once it was established, we could work more easily with many groups to build a program around that set of skills. After three years, we reviewed and revised the list to reflect our changing understanding of the technology goals we wanted our students to achieve. In the newest version (Table 6.1), we have put more emphasis on being able to use representational technologies; consistent with the university's general education requirements, we have also explicitly identified information literacy skills as part of the desired goals.

Identify Desired Outcomes

Another important clarification for a successful program is identifying desired outcomes. This enables development of guidelines for participants about activities appropriate to the program, and it helps everyone know how you intend to measure the success of the program.

Desired outcomes may include improvement of student technology skills, improved academic performance for students, more student satisfaction with academic programs, greater faculty use of

Table 6.1. Technology Goals for George Mason University Students

Students Will Be Able to:	Essential (Examples)	Advanced (Examples)
1. Engage in electronic collaboration	Send and receive e-mail; understand "netiquette"	Participate in collaborative writing; participate in an electronic conference
2. Use and create structured electronic documents	Create, format, and edit a document using a word processing program	Use templates, macros, and mail merge to automate repetitious tasks
3. Do technology-enhanced presentations	Use a presentation software package to create, format, and edit an electronic presentation	Modify standard tools and templates for presentations and develop their own
4. Use electronic tools for research and evaluation	Understand and apply search strategies appropriate to the Web and on-line databases	Select databases and other resources according to discipline, timeliness, and coverage
5. Use databases to manage information	Enter data into a preexisting database; conduct simple queries of a database	Set up a relational database of two or three tables; construct a query for a simple relational database
6. Use spreadsheets to manage information	Enter data into a new or existing spreadsheet; format the layout of a spreadsheet	Use templates and macros to automate repetitious tasks; use statistical, logical, and financial formulas
7. Use electronic tools for analyzing qualitative and quantitative data	Use a statistical package to enter data, name variables, and define variable values	Perform reliability and validity analyses
8. Use graphical and multimedia representational technologies	Perform simple manipulations on existing images (download, resize, crop, change format)	Add special effects to an image (color, lighting, reverse, etc.)

Table 6.1. *(continued)*

Students Will Be Able to:	Essential (Examples)	Advanced (Examples)
9. Demonstrate familiarity with major legal, ethical, privacy, and security issues in information technology	Understand the basics of copyright and property law as they apply to electronic materials	Understand the ethical issues raised by artificial intelligence, virtual reality, etc.
10. Have a working knowledge of hardware and software	Perform basic computer operations on at least one computer platform	Install basic peripheral devices (printer, scanner, etc.)

technology, better job placement for graduates, or an enhanced reputation for the institution in an area of strategic importance to it. Outcomes can also focus on building a specific partnership with the business community or with another college or university in the region or beyond.

With TAC, George Mason's primary desired outcome is that every student graduates from the university with a range of technology skills based on the program's goals. As we revised those technology goals, we added specific performance descriptions so that faculty who were redesigning a course would know what kind of assignment—encompassing both technology fluency and information literacy as appropriate—they would need to build in. Taking the domain of technology fluency as an example, the first definition of the technology goals indicated that graduates would be able to use a spreadsheet; in our revised version, we have specified more exactly what they need to be able to do with a spreadsheet in a beginning or general education course and what they need to be able to do with one in an advanced course in the major. (See Table 6.1 for examples of essential and advanced performance in each goal area.)

This focus on student achievement and student learning means that TAC does not fund proposals that focus on faculty delivery of instruction. At another institution, delivery of instruction may be an important step in achieving the goals of the program and thus well worth funding.

Identify Resources

Armed with understanding of exactly what you want to achieve, you must find existing resources or develop new ones that can help you meet your institution's goals. Take another look at that list of stakeholders and see what financial, personnel, or organizational resources they might have that can help build your proposed program. The more your program's goals align with the goals and interests of potential stakeholders, the more likely they are to share or contribute resources. The availability of resources may determine priorities for implementing the program.

In higher education, leveraging existing resources is an effective, time-honored strategy. If the provost, dean, department chair, chief librarian, head of student services, or development office supports your initiative, then you may be able to take advantage of funding already available for such purposes as curriculum development, faculty and staff development, workforce development, or even classroom renovation. Or you may be able to use these funds to interest a business partner, state or local government, or a foundation in helping implement your project. If funds aren't available to accomplish everything you want, then target one part of the project whose success is assured and that is highly likely to engender additional funding. In some institutions, technology enhancement may be considered to add value to the educational experience, so students and their parents pay an extra technology fee or buy a computer for student use.

Likewise, the more the program can build on existing staff and existing organizational structures, the easier it is to implement. Is there an organizational or administrative structure in place at your institution that can manage this program? The goals of the program determine to a certain extent how elaborate a structure you need. If the program involves distributing money, then part of the administration has to be an institutional agent with fiscal authority. If the program is built as part of the regular faculty teaching load and no extra money is involved, then perhaps an existing academic committee structure at the departmental, school or college, or institutional level, as appropriate, can review and approve curricular changes that meet the program goals.

In implementing TAC, George Mason University did create a few new structures (such as hiring a coordinator for the program and bringing together a number of technology support services into one unit), but as much as possible we used the existing resources and organizational structure of the College of Arts and Sciences and the Information Technology unit, the two principle partners in the initiative. When the university libraries began to restructure their instruction program with an information literacy focus, discussion began immediately to see how we could collaborate and help each other achieve mutual goals. When the university added an IT proficiency component to its general education requirements, we worked closely with the universitywide general education committee to make sure that the TAC program was in harmony with general education goals and that the committee was aware of the TAC and library goals in planning its implementation.

Check Your Technology Infrastructure

A program to enhance student technology learning needs technology resources and may flounder if they are not readily available. It can be extremely frustrating to plan new ways to get students and faculty to use technology, only to discover that there are few facilities on campus where they can learn or use these skills, or that the network or server capacity is insufficient to support your plans, or that the technology cannot be accessed when and where it is needed, or that insufficient networked digital scholarly resources are available. It is wise to start with an understanding of your institution's existing technology infrastructure and any plans already in place to enhance that infrastructure. Working with your IT staff and librarians, you may be able to target improvements in the areas most important to your program.

Besides looking at the existing structure, you should also take into account whatever increased demand for technology resources your program may generate. Once people start using certain kinds of technology in instruction, more faculty and students want to use them, and expectations grow. Not only do they want to do electronic presentations in every classroom; now they want electronic presentations with audio and video clips accessible over the network. If there's no possibility that the institution can make that level of technology available, then you must manage expectations or else risk seeing your program labeled as a failure even as it succeeds.

In the case of TAC, we had two major concerns about technology. Faculty wanted to be sure that students would be supported in learning technology skills outside of the classroom and that there would be enough technology-enhanced classrooms to allow faculty and students to demonstrate the targeted technology skills. We dedicated part of the IT staff to the task of mentoring students in technology skills; we focused our equipment funds on making more classroom technology available.

Build Your Support Team

New curricula using technology require planning on how you will support the students and the faculty who are to use that technology. Faculty support may include financial incentives or release time as well as student assistants, professional staff trained in instructional design and instructional technology, training classes in instructional technology, librarians to consult regarding research assignments and resources, printed and on-line resource materials, models of the kind of assignment or evaluation you want them to use, and peer mentors.

Students likewise need a range of support if they are expected to use technology in new ways as part of their learning process. Except for those in some technical disciplines, faculty generally do not want to dedicate class time for teaching technology skills or information literacy. So although they may expect students to be able to create an electronic presentation for class, they are not going to spend class time teaching this application. Likewise, they may not devote instructional time to the process of conducting topical literature research and reporting of findings. Students who need it must be able to get the basics of these skills somewhere else. How will your institution facilitate this? Perhaps you can offer short training sessions through one of the technology-related academic departments. Perhaps you can include this kind of training in instructional sessions held by the library or IT staff.

In the TAC program, we made use of existing instructional support staff (and librarians when appropriate) to work with faculty in developing and implementing course revision proposals. We also developed a new program to make available graduate and undergraduate student assistants for technology projects. In addition, we expanded an existing student technology facility to include a broader range of support and licensed on-line instructional modules for several hundred software applications.

Develop an Assessment Plan

Assessment constitutes a key feature of educational endeavors. In practical terms, it helps you to keep on improving your program and assures your participants and funders that the program is doing what was intended. Therefore, think early on about how you will show that the program is achieving its outcomes.

Can you repurpose data that are already being collected at the institution, as through graduating senior or alumni surveys that ask about student use of technology during or after their educational experience? Or do you need to collect new sets of data? Perhaps you can work with admissions or student services to collect benchmark information about the technology and associated skills students bring with them to the institution.

It is also important to work with the faculty who are teaching technology-enhanced courses so that they find ways to assess how students' skills change or how their learning changes as a result of introducing technology or information literacy skills development. You may also want to look at specific tests of competency for all students or a random sample of students to demonstrate the impact of your program.

The organizational structure of the program should include provision for how assessment data are collected and disseminated. Whoever is managing the program has to develop regular reports about how many students and faculty in which areas of the institution participate in the program, and collect data from faculty and other sources about its impact. In addition, thought should be given to how data are applied to improve the program. Who is empowered to make adjustments to it? What are the processes for changing the program?

In our TAC program, we began with a focus on the faculty who were redesigning the curriculum. Proposal guidelines called for inclusion of an assessment component. We didn't always get one, and we spent a lot of time helping faculty to develop that component, including recruiting the head of institutional assessment to give workshops in assessment strategies. But we kept right on asking for those assessment plans and assessment reports until we got results.

We also developed some programmatic strategies for tracking data, such as a grid of which courses included which technology skills; we published regular reports about the number of students, faculty, and departments participating in the program. The leadership of the program also had operational authority to implement change as a result of assessment information.

Think Programmatically

Curricular change is most effective when it is programmatic rather than episodic. If curricular change is left to each individual faculty member to implement, the institution is unlikely to be in a position to know if the end result matches the original intention. With technology fluency and information literacy skills in particular, it is critical to plan for building a range of skills across a number of courses; this can't happen unless there is programwide thinking about the connections between one set of skills and other more advanced ones.

Instead of asking individual faculty to think about technology in their individual courses, consider asking all faculty who teach a particular course to set technology or information literacy goals for the course. That way, every student who takes the course, no matter who teaches it, is working toward the same outcomes as the other students are. If the faculty know, for example, that every first-year biology student uses spreadsheets to accomplish certain tasks, then faculty teaching more advanced courses can build on that to help students use spreadsheets for sophisticated data collection and analysis. If use of spreadsheets in the first year is only hit-or-miss, depending on who is teaching the class, then it is difficult for faculty in other courses to build in advanced uses.

Similarly, developing information literacy skills is a gradual and cumulative process. Abilities and skills acquired early on, beginning with introductory or general courses, serve students well in the courses (including capstone) of their chosen major.

George Mason's TAC program offered extra incentives for group and departmental proposals to encourage the broadest possible collaboration and development across an entire program of study.

If your program is built around a single technology course for all students, then it is important that all faculty be aware of the skills introduced in that course so they can give students additional practice in using the skills in other courses later in their program of study.

If there is no program for ensuring that students use a range of technology and information literacy skills, then they will probably be reintroduced to the same basic skills over and over—never having the opportunity to develop or use more advanced skills at all. In the TAC initiative, for example, we got many proposals for introducing students to Internet research and Web page design, but far fewer that focused on using spreadsheets or electronic presentations, making critical assessment of information and its sources and incorporating selected information in students' written projects, or understanding legal and ethical issues in technology use. We were able to use our tracking grid and our request for proposals to encourage course development across the whole range of skills that we wanted our students to learn (Agee and Holisky, 2000).

Think Collaboratively

Thinking collaboratively may be the most important strategy in working on your project. Terry O'Banion (1997) sets forth a model that is particularly relevant when applied to curriculum development: "Everyone employed in the learning college will be a learning facilitator, including categories formerly designated administration and support or clerical staff. . . . The goal is to have every employee . . . thinking about how his or her work facilitates the learning process" (p. 58).

If the job of helping students develop interrelated technology fluency and information literacy is left to any one group—faculty, librarians, IT staff, career services—then many opportunities are lost. Understanding and using information and information technology is a multifaceted process that can be facilitated from many perspectives. The more the goal of helping students in that process pervades the institution, the more opportunities students have to learn and hone their skills in these areas. Building as large a community of interest as possible brings more resources to bear and allows them to be used most productively.

If an academic department can share instructional materials, directly or indirectly, then it can avoid duplicating work that is being done in other departments. For example, if many departments are introducing spreadsheets or electronic presentations into their courses, there is really no need for every one of them to develop independent tutorials, assignments, evaluation instruments, and so forth. The same holds true for courses incorporating assignments related to information literacy. At the least, if faculty members see what other colleagues have prepared, they can build on each other's work. At best, faculty from several departments might collaborate, assisted by librarians and instructional technologists, in building a library of assignments or tutorials or other instructional resources from which they all can draw.

The TAC program builds on a collaborative relationship between the College of Arts and Sciences and the Information Technology Unit (ITU)—including increasingly the libraries, which are an administrative component of ITU—that involves shared goal setting, shared decisions about priorities and resource allocation, and shared commitment to student learning and success.

Collaborative partnerships can also extend outside the institution— for example, with the business community—in developing internships that help students practice information and technology skills.

Conclusion

No single approach, no single strategy necessarily ensures a successful program that aims to expand and enhance the information literacy and technology fluency of students. A combination of factors, some of which may be unique to a given institution, have to be considered in defining a specific program that helps students at your institution become the information- and technology-savvy citizens and workforce our society needs.

References

Agee, A. S., and Holisky, D. A. "Technology Across the Curriculum at George Mason University." *EDUCAUSE Quarterly*, 2000, *23*(4), 6–12. [www.educause.edu./ir/library/pdf/EQM0041.pdf]

Association of College and Research Libraries. *Information Literacy Competency Standards for Higher Education*. Chicago: Association of College and Research Libraries, 2000. [www.ala.org/acrl/ilcomstan.html]

National Research Council, Committee on Information Technology Literacy. *Being Fluent with Information Technology*. Washington, D.C.: National Academy Press, 1999. [books.nap.edu/books/030906399X/html/index.html]

O'Banion, T. *A Learning College for the 21st Century*. Phoenix: American Council on Education and Oryx Press, 1997.

7

Economic Development
Partnerships to Close the Gap

Annie Hunt Burriss, William H. Wallace, Jr.

Over the past two decades, there has been unprecedented growth in the nation's information technology (IT) industry. With the introduction of the Internet and e-commerce, the pace of this growth has dramatically increased. In 1998, William Valdez, senior policy adviser for the U.S. Office of Science and Technology, said that "the fuel for the new economy is new technology, and the fuel for the new technology is the workforce" (*Help Wanted*, 1998, p. 28).

Of the issues identified by the business community relative to its economic viability and market competitiveness, the most important factor considered was the current and future availability of a qualified, skilled, and educated workforce. Higher education gives the business community an opportunity to access and benefit from its advancements in research and knowledge.

Colleges and universities have emerged as important economic development incubators for intellectual capital. For example, the University System of Georgia (USG) has adopted this strategic position statement: "Intellectual capital is the business capital of the future.®" The University System of Missouri clearly articulated the importance of linking higher education and economic development in its 1999 strategic plan: "Public officials will increasingly rely on universities, especially publicly supported institutions, as instruments of economic growth and development. . . . In the future, universities will play an expanded role in enhancing economic productivity by increasing their participation in knowledge development, technology transfer, and economic policy development. The pressure on universities to foster economic development will require institutions to develop new partnerships that cut across organizations and agencies" (University of Missouri System, 1999).

Astute leaders have historically sought a strong ROI (return on investment). As we continue to migrate to a knowledge-based global economy, the new ROI may come to be viewed as a return on intellectual capital.

Partnering to Meet the Demand

The one constant feature that characterizes the information technology industry is rapid change. Hewlett-Packard, a Fortune 500 company, derives more than 75 percent of its revenues from products that are less than two years old (Farley Group, 2000). Expressed differently, Hewlett-Packard essentially replaces its entire product line every three years. What does this mean in terms of developing economic partnerships between higher education and industry?

The IT industry is concerned with obtaining knowledge regarding the current and future availability of a skilled, creative, and educated workforce; it is also concerned about the amount of time required to prepare and graduate such employees. In a period of economic expansion and low unemployment, finding available and trained workers becomes a primary business concern.

National data reveal that occupations in information technology are among the fastest growing and highest paying. A 1999 study conducted by A. T. Kearney found that in the high-technology field "56 percent of the 317,000 high-tech jobs in 2006 will require a four-year degree, while an additional 9 percent will require a two-year degree" (Kearney, 1999, p. 15).

Data such as these would lead one to conclude that there is a significant opportunity for economic development partnership between higher education and the IT industry. Opportunity exists and should be explored if deemed appropriate, but some caution might be required. Analysis of supply and demand in the business sector does not necessarily correspond to supply and demand as defined by higher education.

In 1999, the USG commissioned a study to inventory the capabilities of its thirty-four institutions to educate students in the information technology field. In 2000, the USG had 206,000 degree-seeking students and 410,000 participants in continuing education programs. In 1999, 1,640 students graduated from system institutions with degrees in IT, ranging from the associate's to the doctorate.

If the nation's fourth largest system of higher education is producing fewer than seventeen hundred graduates per academic year with an IT-related degree, how must higher education partner with that industry to produce a sufficient number of graduates to meet the projections identified by Kearney? The data show that when the IT industry considers economic development partnerships with higher education, it is not solely interested in the number of graduates with an IT-related education.

We are witnessing an emerging trend in the recruitment strategies of the IT industry. The Kearney study reached one conclusion that was unexpected, but significant. In a series of interviews, managers from IT-related businesses were asked to identify the skills that would be important to an employee's success on the job. Their collective response was overwhelming. They indicated they wanted adaptable, people-oriented employees with basic communication skills who had the ability to work well on a team.

Higher education produces graduates in information technology, the sciences, and engineering; it also produces graduates with effective communication skills, broad-based liberal arts backgrounds, a sense of strong cultural awareness, and the skills to work well in teams. As discussed in several previous chapters in this book, workers with skills and capabilities of this sort are also desirable to businesses today.

Attracting Digital-Age Industry to Your State

Among states that are concerned about workforce shortages and their ability to compete in a technology-based market, much attention and research is devoted to the phenomenon called "brain drain." This refers to students who choose to leave their state of residence to attend college or take a job after college graduation. Retention of intellectual capital is a key factor in attracting IT businesses to your state. One of the most important factors that a business considers when it decides to expand or move to a new site location is the current and future availability of a qualified, skilled, and educated workforce.

Another factor in attracting such businesses is that employees within the IT industry have high standards regarding the kind of community that is acceptable as a place to live. Some examples of the quality-of-life issues that are considered by IT professionals are the availability, accessibility, and frequency of cultural activities; the amount of funding allocated for the arts; the implementation of community planning concepts such as smart growth; the cost and location of housing; and the availability of children's day care (Goldberg, 1999). Employees do not wish to fight traffic and urban sprawl on the trip to work or the grocery store, or in taking their children to school.

Information technology companies often employ a site-selection consulting firm when contemplating a decision regarding relocation or expansion. If a state collects and maintains quantitative data regarding the educational and employment characteristics of its higher education students and alumni, the availability of such information enhances the opportunity for new business economic development partnerships. Prospective businesses are interested in information ranging from the average starting salary of a higher education graduate (by degree and program area) to the location of jobs taken by students after graduation (Ady, 1996).

Model Partnerships in Georgia

Believing that intellectual capital is the business capital of the future, in 1994 the board of regents of the University System of Georgia endorsed the concept of a one-stop point of entry by the business community to its thirty-four colleges and universities. From that concept, the system's economic development program, known as the Intellectual CApital Partnership Program (ICAPP®), was created (see www.icapp.org/about).

ICAPP: A Strategic Link

The central role of ICAPP is broker and catalyst to strategically link Georgia's higher education system with the state's economic development efforts. The number of organizations and entities with which ICAPP collaborates is extensive. Among these entities are the state, national, and international business communities; about 150 chambers of commerce and development authorities located throughout Georgia; the thirty-four institutions of the USG; the office of the governor; and the state departments of industry, trade and tourism, labor, revenue, and technical and adult education, as well as the office of planning and budget.

During its initial five years of existence, 1995–2000, ICAPP focused significantly on the information technology industry. Beginning in 1995, IT professionals were in high demand, yet low supply. It was decided that the USG could play an innovative role in attempting to attract and secure critical positions of this type.

The ICAPP program was conceived and implemented primarily to help the State of Georgia convince Total System Services, an information technology company located in Columbus, that it could successfully expand its operations in Georgia rather than relocating to another state. This corporation was and continues to be one of the state's major employers.

As a result of the success of the ICAPP program in this economic development initiative, Total System Services created fifteen hundred new positions and made a capital investment of $100 million in the state over the subsequent three-year period. The *Wall Street Journal* concluded that one of the most significant economic development projects of 1996 was the retention and expansion of Total System Services within our state (Beall, 1997).

ICAPP Advantage

The centerpiece of this economic development program is ICAPP Advantage. ICAPP Advantage has four key facets: (1) accelerated academic programs, (2) the ability to customize academic degree programs to meet a company's specific workforce needs, (3) expedited allocation of resources to system institutions to produce more college graduates in a selected discipline, and (4) the requirement that a participating company be involved with selecting students and guarantee employment to those who successfully complete the program.

ICAPP Advantage is unique in that it was the first instance of a major higher education system in the United States inviting an IT company to its campuses to assist with developing an educational curriculum for degree-seeking students. Among the companies that have participated in the ICAPP Advantage program are Total System Services, Equifax E-Banking Solutions, AFLAC, CheckFree, Nortel Networks, Internet Security Systems (ISS), ComputerLogic, Core Management, and United Parcel Service (UPS).

From 1996 to 2000, the ICAPP Advantage program received $11.7 million from state appropriations, matched by $5.8 million in corporate support. Some sixty-six hundred new jobs were created, led by the high-end IT jobs of twenty-four hundred Georgians completing their expedited education through ICAPP. In 1998, the Georgia State University Economic Forecasting Center concluded that the state was receiving an ROI greater than fifteen to one in the ICAPP Advantage program just from the resulting increased salaries of its graduates, not even counting new capital investments (Ratajczak, 1998).

In Georgia, as elsewhere, economic development is important to businesses as it helps them succeed, and to government at all levels because it creates tax digest; it is particularly important to education because tax digest funds its programs. As the USG achieves success with these programs, it gains favor with these constituencies.

Benefits and Lessons Learned

The USG has derived many benefits from its special funding initiative through the ICAPP Advantage program. According to the final report of a consultant who performed an evaluation of client satisfaction, the program has raised the awareness among companies and academics of the gap between the classroom and industry. Continuing collaborative partnerships should permit a participating institution to remain current with emerging technologies and processes, as well as reduce the existing technology gap between the classroom and the work setting (White, 2001). ICAPP Advantage allows an institution to secure funding for faculty, equipment, and space in a much shorter time frame than in the past. This has enhanced the credibility and viability of this program among our system institutions.

By knitting companies and colleges closely together, the ICAPP Advantage program is building a successful foundation for future corporate investment. As a company's competitive advantage is built through participation in this program, it is more responsive to requests for additional fiscal support. ICAPP Advantage has expedited the education of IT workers to meet a company's specific workforce needs (White, 2001). As a result, it has drawn some students to colleges and universities who would not have attended otherwise. Some are beginning to call ICAPP "Georgia's second-chance university."

Institutions participating in the program have also learned valuable and important lessons that can benefit others who wish to emulate the model.

First, this type of program works best if the economic partnership is based on the recognition of each participant's needs and capacities.

Second, such a program is not always the appropriate solution to a company's business requirements. For example, situations arise in which new technologies or approaches occur more quickly in the industry than institutions can integrate them into their curriculum.

Third, the program, as it is currently constituted, addresses only a company's need for new workers; it does not address the need for retraining existing employees (White, 2001).

The ongoing challenge for ICAPP is to strategically allocate and leverage resources so that it can continue to pursue several initiatives well, without exceeding the limits of its capacity. Economic development trends and needs change quickly. This program has to continue reinventing itself and adapting to the ever-changing needs of its constituents if it is to remain successful and viable.

Complementary Programs

ICAPP Advantage develops knowledge workers, who are in high demand and low supply, but the need exists for businesses and graduates to communicate with each other regarding immediate and available employment opportunities. In 1999, GeorgiaHire, an online, cost-effective resource available at no charge for employers, became operational. This ICAPP Web site (www.GeorgiaHire.com) enables a business to search USG student and alumni résumés. Employers may use e-mail to directly dispatch information regarding a position opening to students. In its first twenty-eight months of operation, approximately ninety-two hundred employers searched more than eighty-six thousand résumés of students and alumni from Georgia's public colleges and universities.

In 1999, an additional economic development initiative was introduced, called Yamacraw (see www.yamacraw.org). The objective of this program is to position Georgia as a world leader in designing high-bandwidth communications. The Yamacraw initiative is designed to grow high-technology clusters within the state that focus on designing electronics for the communications and computer industries. Cooperating closely with business and industry, eight USG institutions are educating students, adding faculty, changing curricula, and conducting research in broadband communications, optical and wireless networks, high-speed access, and content processing.

What Others Are Doing

A number of initiatives have been established to promote partnership between higher education and the IT industry. As Aspray and Freeman point out in Chapter One, jobs within the IT field require varying skill sets and levels of knowledge. The education and training requirements that are needed by the IT industry are complex, requiring coordination among technical schools, two- and four-year higher education institutions, and graduate school programs.

A good example of a partnership that helps to meet the IT industry's education and training needs is the Applied Information Management (AIM) Institute, established in 1992 as a nonprofit corporation in Omaha, Nebraska (see www.aiminstitute.org). AIM's purpose is to ensure that graduates of academic programs possess the skills needed by the IT industry, that IT workers can remain up to date in their knowledge and skills, and that IT worker availability is improved (Skinner and Cartwright, 1998). AIM members include community colleges, public and private universities, local businesses and corporations, state government, and the local chamber of commerce.

The Commonwealth of Pennsylvania funds a similar project, Information Technology Workforce Development (ITWD), designed to enable higher education institutions in the state to attract, retain, and graduate information technology students with the knowledge and skills that match the needs of Pennsylvania employers. Project partners include eighty-seven businesses, fifty-four educational institutions, and nine government and nonprofit organizations. In addition, last year a new grant called I-Grad provided funding to Pennsylvania colleges and universities that designed programs to target investment in IT disciplines, technology-influenced disciplines, and nontechnology disciplines that explore how technology is changing their field. (For information about these programs, see l2l.org/highered.html.)

The USG surveyed a number of states regarding their respective economic development partnership initiatives. Included in the survey were Alabama, Arizona, California, Illinois, Kentucky, Maryland, Massachusetts, New York, North Carolina, Ohio, Oklahoma, Oregon, Pennsylvania, and South Carolina.

In interviews with representatives from these states, a number of questions were asked regarding the nature and the extent of partnership (Farley Group, 2000). Questions regarding the structure and organization of a state's higher education system were raised. In addition, individuals were asked if there was a single designated office within their state that facilitated access by prospective businesses to its university, two-year college, and other technology resources. If there was no single designated state office, representatives were asked how the resources of their public and private higher education system would be coordinated to respond to interest on the part of an IT business in considering that state as a possible location site.

Most of the states surveyed lacked a single point of access to university resources for a business that was interested in establishing an IT economic development partnership. The Oklahoma University System recently created an Office of System Advancement and Economic Development, apparently to give businesses one-stop access to the resources of its colleges and universities.

According to our survey results, Maryland stands out for its comprehensive approach to business access to services delivered by community colleges and four-year schools. In 1998, the Maryland Applied Information Technology Institute (MAITI) built a partnership that included all four-year public institutions, along with private colleges and universities. In 2000, the MAITI partnership was extended to Maryland's independent community colleges. Simultaneously, the state's education department has developed a career-oriented "clusters" program for grades nine through twelve. It is believed that MAITI's postsecondary partnership will connect its efforts to this program within the next few years.

Ben Franklin Technology Partners is a state-funded economic development program in the Commonwealth of Pennsylvania dedicated to advancing the state's knowledge-based economy. The program is explicitly funded for the purpose of supporting small to medium industries with a high-tech focus, and many of the partnerships are allied to universities in the state. Included in the program is the Pennsylvania Alliance of Higher Education for Research and Technology, which provides an on-line searchable database of faculty, unique equipment, and specialized facilities in colleges and universities that are available as resources for industry, research, and technology development.

The Massachusetts Institute of Technology (MIT) is a private institution with one of the best technology commercialization and entrepreneurial records in the world. Its Industrial Liaison Program is a membership, fee-based service that enables businesses to access a range of structured services. These services include sponsored research programs; one-on-one meetings with faculty to discuss emerging research projects of interest; access to MIT libraries, publications, and related data resources; corporate strategy and management assessments; and participation in courses, seminars, and conferences.

In reviewing the data from each of the states surveyed, we found certain themes and patterns. Economic development networking among institutions and organizations in higher education is becoming more common. IT economic development partnerships between institutions of higher education and corporations follow a range of strategies and approaches.

Most business outreach appears to be centered on technology transfer and the promotion of university research. Conversely, most training or education outreach on behalf of a specific business appears to begin with either a two-year institution or a state workforce development agency.

Although the IT economic development partnership strategies of some states promote workforce development, others favor technology commercialization. For those states promoting both, efforts are not always coordinated. Most of the IT economic development partnerships have been established at the institutional level, rather than statewide (Farley Group, 2000).

Trade publications such as *Expansion Management* (www.expansionmanagement.com) often rate and rank economic development programs of interest. Other resources of interest are *Site Selection* (www.siteselection.com) and the International Economic Development Council (www.iedconline.org), an organization recently formed through the merger of the Council for Urban Economic Development and the American Economic Development Council.

Recommendations

Colleges and universities have a unique opportunity to develop economic development partnerships with the information technology industry and thus reduce the gap between supply and demand for IT workers. There may be considerable agreement that there is a strong linkage between higher education and a community's economic development, but making that connection occur is complex.

Economic development trends and needs change quickly. We recommend that a number of factors be considered when exploring an industry-education partnership:

• *Alliances.* Increasing attention is being focused on promoting industry alliance as an effective economic development tool. States and institutions of higher education should participate in regular business roundtables for industry clusters to identify the skill needs of the industry in that area; select common concerns and issues; and share costs for marketing, employee training, and acquisition of technology and equipment.

- *One-stop access.* The ability of a state to establish a one-stop point of access to the resources of its *public and private* institutions of higher education is attractive to a prospective business.

- *Early interest.* A person's interest in a career in information technology should not begin while attending a college or university. States and institutions of higher education should work with high schools to develop curricula that are designed to prepare the student for a targeted career path. Linking K–12 with the economic development initiatives of a state is next on the horizon.

- *Faculty.* For an institution to produce graduates with the knowledge, skills, and creativity required by the IT industry, faculty must be knowledgeable and skilled in technological issues and applications, as well as have access to the type of equipment needed to use that knowledge.

- *Curriculum.* Curriculum redesign should be more responsive to the growing demand for skilled technicians.

- *Public-private linkage.* Opportunities to link the collective resources of public and private institutions of higher education should be considered to enhance statewide economic development, more so than regional economic development.

- *Hiring versus retraining.* From an IT company's point of view, there is often little distinction between the need for new workers and retraining its existing workforce. The company wants to employ individuals to solve a constantly changing set of challenges and opportunities. Sometimes the appropriate solution is to add workers; sometimes it is to retrain and reassign existing employees. Companies are willing to pay for the cost of instruction, but they need such instruction to be delivered in ways that allow employees to continue to be productive on their present jobs, while they are trained for new jobs (White, 2001).

- *E-learning.* Serious consideration should be given to e-learning as a delivery mechanism for a partnership program. Web-based training is expected to increase more than 100 percent a year and possibly reach $12 billion by 2002 (Boyett, Boyett, Henson, and Spirgi-Hebert, 2001). A number of successful "learning marketspace" partnerships have been established between higher education and industry with a Web site as their focal point (Duin, Baer, and Starke-Meyerring, 2001).

- *Long-term projects.* The most successful higher education and IT industry collaborations for expanding and improving the pool of IT workers tend to be "sustained, multiple-year programs, not short-term projects" (Skinner and Cartwright, 1998, p. 53).

- *Collaboration.* Public officials, higher education governing boards, and corporate leaders must work to remove barriers to collaboration by developing mutually beneficial business plans, rather than colleges and universities looking for grants "up-front" as a precondition of working together (Skinner and Cartwright, 1998).

Simply stated, considerable planning must go into an economic development partnership initiative. Issues of mapping out curriculum, securing instructors, and acquiring facilities and equipment must be considered, and lessons associated with economies of scale have to be kept in mind. The first students to complete the program are the most expensive on a per-student basis. However, each class that follows grows less expensive as faculty and staff are in place, the curriculum is established, and the requisite equipment and space are secured (White, 2001).

Economic development partnerships are extensive and diverse. Higher education is only beginning to realize the potential for partnership to bridge the gap between the supply and demand for information technology workers.

References

Ady, R. "Information Used by Site Selection Firms in Evaluating the Availability of University Graduates." Atlanta: Deloitte & Touche and Fantus Consulting, Nov. 1996.

Beall, P. "Quarterly Review and Outlook: Who Won—and Lost—Jobs." *Wall Street Journal, Southeast Journal,* Jan. 8, 1997, p. S7.

Boyett, J. H., Boyett, J. T., Henson, R., and Spirgi-Hebert, H. *HR in the New Economy: Trends and Leading Practices in Human Resources Management.* PeopleSoft, 2001.

Duin, A., Baer, L., and Starke-Meyerring, D. *Partnering in the Learning Marketspace.* San Francisco: Jossey-Bass, 2001.

Farley Group. *Taking Stock: The Intellectual Capital Partnership Program (ICAPP) of the University System of Georgia.* Atlanta: Farley Group, 2000.

Goldberg, D. "1999 Southern Economic Survey: The Road Ahead." *Atlanta Journal-Constitution,* Apr. 12, 1999, p. E9.

Help Wanted: Building a Competitive Workforce. Proceedings of conference sponsored by Council for Urban Economic Development and Indianapolis Private Industry Council, Indianapolis, 1998.

Kearney, A. T. *Job Skill Imperatives for Georgia's Future.* (Pre-event briefing document.) Atlanta, Nov. 1999.

Ratajczak, D. *Analysis of Georgia's Intellectual Capital Partnership Program.* Atlanta: Economic Forecasting Center, Georgia State University, 1998.

Skinner, R. A., and Cartwright, G. P. "Higher Education and the Technology Workforce Shortage." *Change,* May/June 1998, pp. 52–55.

University of Missouri System. *A Design for the Future.* Columbia: University of Missouri System, 1999.

White, O. *Evaluation of Client Satisfaction with the University System of Georgia's Intellectual Capital Partnership Advantage Program.* Atlanta: Civic Strategies, 2001.

8

Leadership Challenges for the Campus and the Profession

Brian L. Hawkins, Deanna B. Marcum

Cornelius Pings, past president of the Association of American Universities, wrote of the sweeping impact that technology is having on higher education: "The explosive development of digital technology has engaged every sector of the academic community, but the future impact of the technology will be even more sweeping. Digital information technology will profoundly influence the production, dissemination, and management of information; its impact may affect the structure, operation, and governance of the higher education enterprise as well" (1998, p. viii). Although this statement still rings largely true today, the suggestion by Pings that this new technology *may* affect structure, operation, and governance now appears to be a serious understatement.

Clearly, information technology (IT) is having an enormous impact on every dimension of college and university life. The new technologies are profoundly affecting teaching and learning, creating new opportunities and new competitors in the world of distributed learning. E-business strategies are transforming how business transactions are conducted, and interactive on-line student services demand more comprehensive and complex support structures. New technological tools are creating new opportunities for scholarly inquiry; for example, researchers can now visualize complex data sets and collect information in ways that were never possible before. Networks enable real-time collaboration among scholars who may be geographically distant. Increasingly, important issues are arising as to how a college or university presents itself, with more attention paid to Web sites and portal technologies than was ever given to counterpart print materials, largely because of the ubiquity of the Internet.

As they work to integrate information technology into the fabric of their institution, campus leaders are struggling more than ever with structural, operational, and governance issues. Not only is IT transforming how colleges and universities conduct their affairs, but the manner in which digital resources and information technology and services are provided is also changing. Two decades ago, the chief technology administrator on campus was usually the director of a central computer facility. However, with technology everywhere and becoming integral to achieving campus academic and administrative goals, the technology leader has progressed from overseeing a physical facility to helping oversee and assume responsibility for the institution's strategic investment in and effective management of information resources and technology.

The traditional roles of the computer center and the library—and the professionals who have led these organizations—are no longer adequate to support the changed environment. A new kind of leadership—with new sets of skills and orientations—is needed; throughout the institution, various managers of digital resources and information technologies have to assume new roles. This is true whether these leaders are chief information officers (CIOs), chief technology officers, IT directors, librarians, or other high-level administrators with responsibility for managing an institution's digital resources and information technology.

Thus, colleges and universities are challenged not only by the shortage of and competition for the specific technical skill sets needed to advance institutional strategies related to IT but also by the need to ensure effective information technology leadership at the highest levels. This chapter explores new roles for such leadership and recommends some leadership strategies and tactics to fos-

ter effective stewardship of campus information resources and technology in the digital age.

Defining New Leadership Roles

Too many people with functional responsibilities in a higher education institution see themselves solely as advocates for their area
of responsibility. Leaders, on the other hand, see themselves not in
terms of the functional units they head but as part of the institution
as a whole. The leader of an information resource or technology
unit on campus increasingly must be an active participant in the
central administration of the academic enterprise, both to be personally effective and to make the institution effective. This new
leadership approach requires the individual to be a partner in recon-
ceptualizing the institutional mission, articulating a vision, and forging the political alliances necessary to achieve the kind of change
that is required. These new roles have little to do with the skills and
mind-set that the leader might have found critical in an earlier stage
of his or her career. The leader today must know how to move beyond the comfortable realm of technical expertise to tackle the hard
questions—especially "What must the college or university become
to remain successful?"

The information resource and technology leader today needs to
understand that his or her role is no longer that of a specialist but
rather that of a generalist, acting and participating as a critical partner in the central administration of the college or the university. To
do this, the individuals must have at least rudimentary knowledge
of things such as grants and contract administration, endowment
spending policies, intercollegiate athletics, financial aid and tuition
discounting, and myriad other facets of the institution as a whole.
Since all of these issues present problems and challenges, it is imper-
ative that the senior administrative team in the institution be able
to look at all of the needs, weigh the tradeoffs, and make informed
decisions. This mitigates against the notion of advocating solely for

the needs of the "stovepipe" that a given individual may officially represent. The objective must be to find an optimal solution for the institution, not to maximize the advantage for a given unit or set of units. To do the latter is to create a suboptimal solution; the management literature is full of examples in which such solutions have led to poor overall organizational health.

This is a fine line to walk, because leaders are expected to advocate for the functional area that they represent. It is the balance between advocating for special needs and looking out for the larger interests of the institution that ultimately determines the credibility and the respect given to any senior administrator responsible for leading information resources and technology. Is this individual seen as being at the top level of the IT or library organization, or at the bottom level of the central administration? If either role predominates, then the individual is probably not executing the role well, as it is a blend of these two functions that is essential to effective leadership.

Strategies for Effective Leadership

A number of strategies seem to be increasingly important for effective leadership within the broad scope of managing information resources and technology.

Articulate a Vision

One of the fundamental responsibilities incumbent on a CIO, librarian, IT director, or other administrator charged with institutional IT leadership is the ability to articulate a vision clearly. With the rapid changes in higher education, most of which are driven by information technology, it is important to provide a sense of what the future might look like and how it will affect the operations and functions within the academy.

Nobody's crystal ball is going to be entirely accurate, but this vision of the future serves as a yardstick against which to measure the importance of day-to-day concerns, placing them in perspective and allowing other executives in the institution to understand the transitions that are affecting them. Warren Bennis (1989) describes the greatest obstacle to leadership as "being consumed by the routine." It is precisely this routine that cannot and should not dominate discussion of technological change at the college or university. Rather, these conversations need to be shaped and facilitated by someone who can talk about the vision for the institution and its mission, not just about technological innovations per se. Such a leader uses every opportunity possible to share the *why* of the plan so that others understand the bigger picture. The ability to explain what a specific decision or act leads to is often the defining element of a leadership role. Effective information resource and technology leaders tend to think broadly, and they certainly think collaboratively. The vision is based on what *we* can achieve, rather than what *I* can accomplish.

Another dimension of the challenge of articulating a vision is assuming the role of teacher, helping other senior officers of the college or university begin to articulate their own vision of the new opportunity generated by information technology and the communication opportunities that are created by this technology.

Aim to Make a Difference

The head of an organizational unit is concerned about doing his or her job effectively, but for a leader that isn't enough. A leader is also committed to making a difference! An IT leader in particular needs to be driven to make change in fundamental societal and organizational structures. It is the passion for making something better that determines the immediate course of action for that leader. Making a difference is an intrinsic motivation, separate from the public acclaim or rebuke that may be associated with such efforts. It is what keeps real leaders coming back when it would be easier to take a course of much less resistance. This concept is captured succinctly in George Bernard Shaw's famous quote, "Some men see things the way they are and ask, 'Why?' I dream things that never were, and ask, 'Why not?' "

Information resource and technology leaders need to act from an ingrained set of principles that they can define for others. They cannot be satisfied with a strategic plan unless it corresponds with their fundamental principles. This value-driven approach to leadership may, at times, lead to jousting at windmills, so the leader must temper idealism with realism.

Increasingly, these leaders need to be sure that they are focusing on the big issues of high importance to the institution and to themselves personally. Often the issues they choose are controversial because all fundamental innovation by definition violates the status quo; but in the long run, these are the issues most likely to have the greatest influence on the institution. However, all of this requires careful tactical choices; it is important not to get involved in every issue that comes along, nor to fight every battle, because of the ultimate loss of credibility and the diminishing energy level that ensue.

Share and Accept Responsibility

Information resource and technology leaders should help others understand that their job now includes responsibility for managing and leveraging the information and technology assets that fall within their purview. It is no longer acceptable that all IT-related issues be relegated to the chief information officer, chief technology officer, dean of libraries, or whomever the institution has made responsible for information resources and technology. Information technology challenges need to be integrated into the portfolio of all upper-level managers in a college or university, but surely this requires education, tutelage, and encouragement. Occasionally, it means that the leader accepts responsibility for an effort that is not spelled out as part of a job description or even remotely associated with an official role, just because it needs doing for the betterment of the institution. Though there is sometimes danger in that such behavior might be perceived as stepping out of line, more often it is seen as demonstrating commitment to institutional betterment and being a partner in the overall enterprise.

Once a more collective ownership of responsibility is achieved, it is important for information resource and technology leaders to ensure the success of an effort by rallying support and inspiring other members of the community to get behind it. This is just another element in the overall effort to educate and persuade the community to buy into the vision, the objectives, and the rationale for information technology investment.

Understand Yourself

The information resource and technology leader is likely to work with disparate groups on campus. Making change in the institution requires working in a number of ways with constituencies. The ability to work effectively with many groups requires deep personal understanding of both style and approach. It is understanding of one's own style and strengths that makes it possible for the IT leader to work effectively under varying circumstances.

The effective leader understands that each style has advantages and disadvantages. Those who excel at bringing disparate groups together may lead in a quiet way, while others may exercise influence through motivational speeches or finely crafted essays. Some are able to translate the highly specialized language of a technical and academic discipline into general language that is readily adopted by funders and legislators. The most effective leaders know their strengths and surround themselves with others who complement those strengths. The leader understands his or her humanity and effect on other people and therefore acknowledges bias and filtering in discussing problems with others who may see things differently.

Focus on Multiple Constituencies

In assuming any management position, it is important to understand that the position is defined by three sets of roles and relationships: with one's superior, subordinates, and peers. Each individual or constituency has expectations and needs that must be met, and how heavily the manager responds to one or another of these expectations can define—or essentially redefine—the position. Everyone has encountered a person who sucks up to the boss, giving the superior all of the attention and deference in order to ingratiate himself or herself. An effective leader, however, communicates with all of the people with whom she or he interacts with equal respect and care. Too many people believe they can get away with treating the boss well while showing disrespect to others; ultimately they all seem to get caught in this shortsighted approach. Information resource and technology leaders must understand that relationships to the boss, to subordinates, and to peers are all important for institutional success, and the successful leader does not neglect any one of these areas. This approach is perhaps nothing more than an organizational equivalent of the golden rule, but all too many managers (not to be confused with true leaders) fail to comprehend this concept. A leader who has credibility and respect from all sectors of the community can invariably be found to treat all parties in this respectful, communicative, and engaging manner.

Take Risks

Leadership in the new digital environment, almost by definition, means working in a highly uncertain and dynamic environment. There are no safe and secure routes to pursue while practicing leadership. This is an environment in which a leader *must* take risks. This does not imply being careless or foolhardy, but it does mean being willing to chart a course or route that has not been thoroughly tested, rather than relying on one that is comfortable or has always worked in the past. In an environment where technology is everywhere, following established practice is a luxury that leaders can rarely afford. However, it is important for information resource and technology leaders to be able to articulate the risk, the alternatives, and the consequences of inaction as they define a direction for the campus. To do this requires the leader to have one managerial attribute that is scarce on college and university campuses today: courage.

It is also important for leaders not only to be willing to take a risk personally but also to give those around them license to take risks. Recognizing that they are visible and that any mistakes will be quite public, leaders must establish an environment that encourages risk for important issues, providing assurance that individuals who work for and with them will not be victimized for taking risks. Leaders must establish a climate that accepts that failure is bound to occur in such an uncertain environment.

In essence, these leaders need to develop a safety net for their staff, letting them know that trying new approaches and defining new alternatives is something that is rewarded rather than punished. As described already, a key responsibility for leaders in managing information resources and technology today is to share their vision for the future with both institutional leaders and subordinates, inspiring them to have their own vision, and to take appropriate risks to achieve it.

Where Will We Find This New Leadership Talent?

Just where will our colleges and universities find the talent to fill leadership positions that are so critical to accomplishing the institutional mission in the digital age? Most likely, the talent will come from a far wider array of sources than at any time in recent history. In both information technology and librarianship, the traditional career path is less defined today than in the past and possibly not relevant to producing the new kind of leadership that is called for. As already discussed, IT leadership positions now call for a generalist, but everything about the traditional career path has emphasized specialized skills as a route to advancement. Specialist skills do not mitigate against having the perspective of a generalist, but the broader viewpoint must be developed and nurtured throughout a professional career. This has important implications for mentoring within the organization and for the professional development opportunities sought and encouraged outside the institution.

Leadership in information resources and technology increasingly requires the ability to integrate core academic functions with information support and services; consequently, the people filling these positions should have a clear view and be a partner in the educational enterprise. For this reason, we are seeing, and are likely to see more, faculty assuming top leadership positions in information resources and technology. Most of all, however, we must not just seek alternative venues in which to find such leaders; we must actively and consciously try to develop leaders by mentoring the next generation and helping to anticipate the burgeoning need for such talent.

It is this broader institutional perspective and awareness of the influences on the entire higher education enterprise that are much of the focus of the Frye Leadership Institute sponsored by EDUCAUSE, the Council on Library and Information Resources (CLIR), and Emory University. (More information about this program can be found at www.Frye.org.) We believe this effort is an important element in meeting the need for more leaders in this arena, but the current—not to mention anticipated—demand far exceeds the supply, as illustrated by the number of failed searches for CIOs and librarians with the new leadership mind-set and skills through all sectors of the higher education community. It is necessary for the current generation of leaders to tackle more aggressively the challenges of mentoring and preparing a new generation of leaders. This is extremely difficult when facing relentless and sometimes overwhelming challenges; nonetheless this must become a priority for the long-term health of our institutions.

Conclusion

Institutional change will come through the dedicated efforts and hard work of committed leaders. Colleges and universities cannot expect the new generation of leaders to wait patiently for their turn.

The institution must support education and training programs that help talented younger staff find their leadership métier. Programs such as the Frye Leadership Institute help, but one person taking part in a program—even if it is very good—is not enough to create a climate of change on a campus. An environment that encourages experimentation, rewards innovation, and tolerates mistakes is necessary for the young manager to move into a leadership role.

References

Bennis, W. *Why Leaders Can't Lead: The Unconscious Conspiracy Continues*. San Francisco: Jossey-Bass, 1989.

Pings, C. "Foreword." In B. L. Hawkins and P. Battin (eds.), *The Mirage of Continuity: Reconfiguring Academic Information Resources for the 21st Century*. Washington, D.C.: Council on Library and Information Resources and American Association of Universities, 1998.

Index